The Deepfake Dilemma

Safeguarding Institutions and Citizens in the Digital Age

snova
New York

Computer Science, Technology and Applications Series

Smart Decision Systems: Integrating Symbolic AI and Cognitive Heuristics for IOMT
Hemant Kumar Saini, PhD, Christian Kaunert, and Bhupinder Singh
ISBN: 979-8-89530-935-3
eBook ISBN: 979-8-89530-993-3

Artificial Intelligence: Policy Perspectives and Global Impacts
Sonja Buckley (Editor)
ISBN: 979-8-89530-859-2
eBook ISBN: 979-8-89530-960-5

Immersive Technologies: The Role of Augmented and Virtual Reality in Civilian and Military Use
Rosalie T. Bryant (Editor)
ISBN: 979-8-89530-796-0
eBook ISBN: 979-8-89530-910-0

The Future of Machine Learning with Automation in Engineering
Sandeep Gupta, PhD
ISBN: 979-8-89530-556-0
eBook ISBN: 979-8-89530-607-9

Big Data, Big Impact: Navigating Competition, Privacy, and Reform
Jessica Andrews (Editor)
ISBN: 979-8-89530-538-6
eBook ISBN: 979-8-89530-565-2

Computational Arts and Creative Products: Languages, Spaces and Practices
Alessandra Micalizzi, PhD
ISBN: 979-8-89530-426-6
eBook ISBN: 979-8-89530-499-0

More information about this series can be found at
https://novapublishers.com/product-category/series/computer-science-technology-and-applications/

Ruben Faulkner
Editor

The Deepfake Dilemma

Safeguarding Institutions and Citizens in the Digital Age

snova
New York

Library of Congress Cataloging-in-Publication Data

ISBN: 979-8-90134-122-3 (Softcover)
ISBN: 979-8-90134-143-8 (eBook)

Published by Nova Science Publishers, Inc. † New York

Contents

Preface		vii
Chapter 1	**Advances in Deepfake Technology** Committee on Oversight and Accountability	1
Chapter 2	**Addressing Real Harm Done by Deepfakes** Committee on Oversight and Accountability	27
Chapter 3	**To Protect National Security Against the Threats Posed by Deepfake Technology and to Provide Legal Recourse to Victims of Harmful Deepfakes** Committee on the Judiciary, Committee on Energy and Commerce, and the Committee on Homeland Security	61
Chapter 4	**Deep Fakes and National Security** Laurie A. Harris	77
Chapter 5	**Combating Deepfakes** U.S. Government Accountability Office	83
Chapter 6	**Tools to Address Known Exploitation by Immobilizing Technological Deepfakes on Websites and Networks Act** Committee on Energy and Commerce	89
Chapter 7	**Deepfake Task Force Act** Committee on Homeland Security and Governmental Affairs	113
Index		119

Preface

This volume offers a comprehensive examination of the rapid advancement of deepfake technology and its profound implications for national security, public trust, and individual rights. Drawing from congressional reports, expert testimony, and legislative analysis, it presents a critical assessment of the threats posed by synthetic media and explores the multifaceted legal, policy, and technological strategies being developed to counteract them.

Chapter 1

Advances in Deepfake Technology*

Committee on Oversight and Accountability

Wednesday, November 8, 2023
House of Representatives Committee on Oversight and Accountability
Subcommittee on Cybersecurity, Information Technology,
and Government Innovation
Washington, D.C.

The Subcommittee met, pursuant to notice, at 3:41 p.m., in room 2154, Rayburn House Office Building, Hon. Nancy Mace [Chairwoman of the Subcommittee] presiding.

Present: Representatives Mace, Timmons, Burchett, Langworthy, Burlison, and Connolly.

Ms. MACE. Good afternoon, everyone. The Subcommittee on Cybersecurity, Information Technology, and Government Innovation will come to order.

Welcome, everyone, and without objection, the Chair may declare a recess at any time.

I recognize myself for the purpose of making an opening statement.

Good afternoon, and welcome to this hearing of the Subcommittee on Cybersecurity, Information Technology, and Government Innovation.

The groundbreaking power of artificial intelligence is a double-edged sword. That is nowhere more evident than in AI's capacity to generate

* This is an edited, reformatted and augmented version of Hearing Before the Subcommittee on Cybersecurity, Information Technology, and Government Innovation of the Committee on Oversight and Accountability House of Representatives, One Hundred Eighteenth Congress, First Session, Serial No. 118–74, dated November 8, 2023.

In: The Deepfake Dilemma
Editor: Ruben Faulkner
ISBN: 979-8-90134-122-3

realistic-looking images, audio, and video. The latest AI algorithms can be used to make synthetic creations nearly indistinguishable from actual faces, voices, and events. These creations are referred to as deepfakes.

Deepfakes can be put to a variety of productive uses. They are used to enhance video games and other forms of entertainment, and they are being used to advance medical research as well, but deepfake technology can also be weaponized and cause great harm. It can be used to make people appear to say or do things that they have not said or done. It can be used to perpetuate various crimes, including financial fraud and intellectual property theft. It can also be used by anti-American actors to create national security threats, and these are not hypothetical harms.

It must be me today.

OK. A few weeks ago, AI-generated pornographic images of female students at a New Jersey high school were circulated by male classmates. A company that studies deepfakes found more than 90 percent of deepfake images are pornographic. Last month, the attorneys general of 54 states and territories wrote to congressional leaders urging they address how AI is being used to exploit children, specifically through the generation of child sexual abuse material, or CSAM, pronounced ''Cee-Sam.'' They wrote, ''AI can combine data from photographs of both abused and non-abused children to animate new and realistic sexualized images of children who do not exist but may resemble actual children. Creating these images is easier than ever,'' the letter states, ''as anyone can download the AI tools to their computer and create images by simply typing in a short description of what the user wants to see.'' Falsified videos and photos circulating on social media are also making it difficult to separate fact from fiction in conflicts taking place around the world. Videos purportedly taken from the ground in Israel, Gaza, and Ukraine have circulated rapidly around on social media, only to be proven inauthentic. One AI-generated clip showed the President of Ukraine urging troops to put down their arms. I am not interested in banning all synthetic images or videos that offend some people or make them feel uncomfortable, but if we cannot separate truth from fiction, we cannot ensure our laws are enforced or that our national security is preserved. And there is more insidious danger that the sheer volume of impersonations and false images we are exposed to on social media lead us to no longer recognize reality when it is staring us right in the face.

Bad actors are rewarded when people think everything is fake, thus called the liar's dividend. The classic case of the liar's dividend is the very real hunter Biden laptop, which many in the media and elsewhere falsely attributed to

Russian disinformation, but the risk from deepfakes can be mitigated. We will hear about one such effort today being pursued by a partnership of tech companies interested in maintaining a flow of trusted content. Voluntary standards can enable creators to embed content provenance data into an image or video, allowing others to know if the content is computer generated or has been manipulated in any way.

Our witnesses today will be able to discuss these standards, along with other ideas, for addressing the potential harms caused by deepfakes. With that, I would like to yield to the Ranking Member of the Subcommittee, my friend, Mr. Connolly.

Mr. CONNOLLY. Thank you, Madam Chairwoman, and thank you for having this hearing. Very timely. I will begin by noting our disappointment on the Minority side, yet again, the lack of a hearing on the scorecard for implementation of FITARA. This Committee initiated that legislation, created that scorecard, has had 15 hearings—a record for Congress—and it has produced over $25 billion of savings. We believe strongly that we need to continue that oversight and continue to press the executive branch for progress. I would note that until now, that effort over the last 7 years has been completely bipartisan. I have worked with my colleagues on the other side of the aisle—Mr. Meadows, Mr. Issa, Mr. Hice, Mr. Hurd—to make this happen, and we have always collaborated in a bipartisan way to make it happen. So, I hope we can revisit that issue and continue to make progress and keep what I think is a very proud record by this Subcommittee and by the full Committee in holding the executive branch's feet to the fire when it comes to IT modernization, updating cybersecurity encryption, and moving to the cloud.

[Slides shown]

Mr. CONNOLLY. With that, with respect to this hearing, when most people hear the term ''deepfake,'' this image may jump to mind. While images like this, His Holiness, Pope Francis, in a puffy coat, seems innocuous, most are, as the Chairwoman just indicated, quite insidious. Take the AI-generated image, for example, the Gaza image on the screen. Since the armed conflict between Israel and Hamas first broke out, false images created by generative technology have proliferated throughout the internet. As a result, these synthetic images have created an algorithmically driven fog of war, making it significantly more difficult to differentiate between truth and fiction. Just last year, at the outset of Russia's invasion of Ukraine, a fabricated video of Ukrainian President Zelensky calling for Ukrainian soldiers to lay down their weapons, also referenced by the Chairwoman, circulated on social media very widely. It was a deepfake, but thanks to Ukraine's quick response to Russian disinformation, it was quickly debunked. Welcome to the new frontier of disinformation.

Politics are one realm of deepfakes, but let us look at some numbers. According to one study, 96 percent of deepfake videos are of non-consensual pornography—96 percent. Another report confirmed that deepfake pornography almost exclusively targets and harms young women. Knowing this, it should be no surprise that the very first deepfake ever created depicted the face of a famous female celebrity superimposed onto the body of an actor in a pornographic video. These kinds of manipulated videos are already affecting students in our schools. In one instance, a group of high school students in New Jersey used the images of a dozen female classmates to make AI pornography. This is wrong. It threatens lives and self-esteem among young people, and it needs to be stopped.

Earlier this year, Ranking Member, Joe Morelle, introduced a bill called the Preventing Deepfakes of Intimate Images Act. The bill bans non-consensual images. The order instructs the Secretary of Commerce—whoops, I am sorry—of sharing synthetic intimate images and creates additional legal courses of action for those who are affected. I am a co-sponsor of that legislation and urge all of my colleagues to join us in this important effort.

Congress must not shy away from preventing harmful proliferation of deepfake pornography, but it is not just deepfake videos that we have to worry about. With AI, scammers have the ability to easily create audio that mimics a person's voice, matching, age, gender, and tone. Thousands of Americans are scammed over the telephone every year using this very technology, and deepfake capabilities further exacerbate the problem. So, what can we do? AI image detecting tools are being developed and used to help verify the authenticity of machine-generated images. Other tools place watermarks on AI-generated media to indicate that the media is synthetically created.

While these tools improve and evolve, both the public and the private sector must cooperate to educate the public on where these tools are and how to use them. Government and the private sector must collaboratively highlight the dangers and consequences of deepfakes and teach how to combat this misinformation and its abuse. Private developers must implement policies that preserve the integrity of truth and to provide transparency to users. That is why I joined the letter, led by Representative Kilmer and the New Democratic Coalition AI Working Group, that requests leaders of prominent, generative AI and social media platforms to provide information to Congress outlining efforts to monitor, identify, and disclose deceptive synthetic media content, and the public sector is already taking bold, consequential steps toward collaboration and comprehensive solutions.

I applaud the efforts of the Biden Administration to secure commitments from seven major AI companies to help users identify when content is, in fact, AI generated and when it is not. The Biden Administration took a resolute and unprecedented step last week when it issued its executive order on artificial intelligence. The sweeping executive order speaks directly to the issues we seek to examine today. It leans on tools, like watermarking, that can help people identify whether what they are looking at online is authentic as a government document or tool of disinformation. The order instructs the Secretary of Commerce to work enterprise-wide to develop standards and best practices for detecting fake content and tracking the provenance of authentic information. I trust this Subcommittee will conduct meaningful oversight of these efforts because we, as a Nation, need to get this right.

I am proud that the Administration has taken the first step in performing its role as a global leader in addressing generative technology. I also look forward to hearing more today about existing and evolving private sector solutions and suggestions. We already know Congress must continue to fund essential research programs that support the development of more advanced and effective deepfake detection tools. Funding for research through DARPA and the National Science Foundation is critical. That requires a fully funded government. I once again urge all of my colleagues on this and the other side of the aisle to fulfill our constitutional duty and work with us to pass a bipartisan, long-term funding agreement.

I thank the Chairwoman, Ms. Mace, for holding this hearing and emphasizing the harm of deepfakes and disinformation, and I look forward to any legislative action that may follow this endeavor. I yield back.

Ms. MACE. Thank you, Mr. Connolly. Today, I am pleased to introduce our witnesses for today's hearing. Our first witness is Mr. Mounir Ibrahim, Executive Vice President of Public Affairs and Impact at Truepic. I would like to next introduce Mr. Langworthy to introduce the second witness.

Mr. LANGWORTHY. Thank you very much, Madam Chair. I am pleased to have the opportunity to introduce our witness from Western New York. Dr. David Doermann is the interim Chair of the Department of Computer Science and Engineering at the State University of New York at Buffalo. He is also a professor of empire innovation and the Director of the Artificial Intelligence Institute at UB. Prior to UB, Dr. Doermann was a program manager at the Defense Advanced Research Projects Agency, or DARPA, where he developed and oversaw $150,000,000 in research funding in the areas of computer vision, human language, and voice analytics technologies. Dr. Doermann is a leading researcher and innovative thinker in the areas of document image analysis and recognition. Welcome to the hearing, Dr. Doermann. We look forward to your testimony today, and I yield back.

Ms. MACE. Thank you. Our third witness is Mr. Sam Gregory, executive director of WITNESS, and our fourth witness today is Mr. Spencer Overton, professor of law at George Washington University School of Law. Welcome, everyone, and we are pleased to have you here this afternoon.

Pursuant to Committee Rule 9(g), the witnesses will please stand and raise your right hands.

Do you solemnly swear or affirm that the testimony you are about to give is the truth, the whole truth, and nothing but the truth, so help you God?

[A chorus of ayes.]

Ms. MACE. Let the record show the witnesses all answered in the affirmative. We appreciate all of you being here today and look forward to your testimony.

Let me remind the witnesses that we have read your written statements, and they will appear in full in the hearing record. Please limit your oral statements to 5 minutes. As a reminder, please press the button on the microphone in front of you so that it is on, and the Members can hear you. When you begin to speak, the light in front of you will turn green. After 4 minutes, the light will turn yellow. When the red light comes up, your 5 minutes has expired, and we would ask that you please wrap it up.

I would like to recognize Mr. Ibrahim to please begin his opening statement.

Statement of Mounir Ibrahim
Vice President of Public Affairs and Impact Truepic

Mr. IBRAHIM. Thank you, Chairwoman Mace, Ranking Member Connolly, and Members of this Subcommittee for the opportunity to brief today. My name is Mounir Ibrahim, Executive Vice President for Truepic, a technology company that focuses on digital content transparency and authenticity. Prior to my time at Truepic, I was a Foreign Service officer with the U.S.

Department of State. My time as a U.S. diplomat was one of the greatest honors of my life and led me to my work today.

I was posted at the U.S. Embassy in Damascus at the start of the Arab Spring. I saw protesters risk their lives, being beaten and attacked in front of me, as they attempted to document the violence with smartphones. It was there I saw the power of user-generated content. Later, as an advisor to two different U.S. permanent representatives to the United Nations, I saw similar images from conflict zones around the world enter into the U.N. Security Council, but regularly undermined by countries, critics, and bad actors that wanted to undermine reality by simply claiming those images were fake. Today, that strategy, as the Congresswoman noted, is referred to as the liar's dividend, and it is highly effective, simply claiming user-generated content is fake.

In my opinion, in addition to the horrible, non-consensual pornographic threat that we have from generative AI, the liar's dividend is one of the biggest challenges we have because we have digitized our entire existence. Government, business, and people all rely on what we see and hear online to make decisions. We need transparency and authenticity in that content to make accurate decisions. There is no silver bullet to transparency or authenticity online, but there is growing consensus that adding transparency to digital content so that content consumers—the people who are seeing those images and videos—can tell what is authentic, what is edited, or what is synthetic, will help mitigate the challenges.

A lot of this work is taking place by a coalition of organizations known as the Coalition for Content Provenance and Authenticity, C2PA, by which Truepic is a proud member. The C2PA developed the world's first open standard for digital content provenance, which is often referred to as content credentials. The basic concept of provenance is attaching the fact or history of that image, that video, that audio that you are interacting with online to the file itself, so the content consumer is informed of the artifacts associated with that, like time, date, how it was created, how it was edited, et cetera. The standard is interoperable, which is critical, so digital content can flow from one platform, one device to another so as long as they align to the same standard.

Truepic supports the C2PA because we believe interoperability is critical to help mitigate the challenges that you all laid out today. Our technology and our approach boils down into two areas: we help secure what is, in fact, authentic and captured from a smartphone, and we help add transparency to a synthetic or generative piece that is created from a platform.

From the authentic side, we created a technology called Secure Controlled Capture. It is used by hundreds of businesses every day, ranging from Equifax to Ford Motor Company, to add transparency into their operations. It has also been used in 150 countries. We have deployed this technology on the ground in Ukraine with Microsoft to help USAID partners document destruction to cultural heritage and national infrastructure. On the generative AI side, the C2PA standard has been recognized by the Partnership for AI as one of the lead disclosure mechanisms for generative AI. We are also a proud supporter of the Partnership for AI, and we strive to work toward this goal.

In April, we worked with Nina Schick, an author, and Revel.ai, to launch the world's first transparent deepfake so when you actually see the video, you see the content credentials and know it is, in fact, generated by AI. This past month, we launched two other partnerships with Hugging Face to democratize these tools to add content credentials so anyone can use them on their open-source models, and with Qualcomm, the chipset manufacturer. We think that is a watershed innovation because generative AI is going to move to your smartphone, and this chipset has this transparency technology added to it. It is worth noting that it is not only Truepic working on this. Microsoft, Adobe, Stability AI have all either launched products or made commitments to add the same transparency. This is a growing ecosystem.

In closing, if possible, I would like to offer some thoughts on how government might help mitigate these AI challenges with transparency and authenticity in mind. First, government has a unique platform, and I applaud you for having this hearing. Events like this will raise awareness and help educate the public and give an opportunity to ask the right questions. Second, legislation can be powerful. We have seen in the National Defense Authorization Act, the bipartisan Deepfake Task Force Act, and the recent Executive Order Section 4.5, all of which point to transparency and authenticity in digital content. We have also seen it abroad in the U.K. and the EU. Finally, government should consider how it can use content credentials to authenticate its own communications and prevent constituents from being deceived, and also reap the same benefits that the private sector does in cost reductions, risk reductions, and fraud reductions.

Thank you for your time, and I welcome any questions.

Ms. MACE. Thank you. I now recognize Mr. Doermann to please begin his opening statement.

Statement of Dr. David Doermann Interim Chair Computer Science and Engineering State University of New York at Buffalo

Mr. DOERMANN. Chairwoman Mace, Ranking Member Connolly, and honorable Members of Congress, I appreciate the opportunity to testify before you today on the pressing issue of deepfake technology, creating and distributing computer-generated images, and voice cloning.

In 2014, only a decade ago, when DARPA began the Media Forensics Program, commonly known as MediFor, the primary goal was to detect and characterize image manipulation at scale. This was consistent with DARPA's mission of preventing strategic surprise. Although we imagined a world where our adversaries would become better at manipulating images, few imagined the pace at which automated manipulation would develop and the impact the technology would have on our society as a whole. The introduction of generative adversarial networks, or GANs, kicked off a plethora of tools that can generate images of people and objects that do not exist, synthesize speech that clones voices of others, implements real-time puppeteering to control talking heads, and, as we hear most, the ability to generate deepfake videos. The surprise we missed perhaps is the automated tools that are becoming more accessible and user friendly. They require a lot less data and a lot less technical expertise. Open-source software can be downloaded today and run by any one of us on a commodity laptop.

As these technologies advance at an unprecedented rate, it is crucial to recognize the potential for both positive and negative implications. We hear its use at both ends of the spectrum every week. This week we heard about AI being used to finish a new Beatles song and, as we have heard from the Ranking Member and Chairwoman, that a group of students in a New Jersey high school used it to generate pornographic videos of their classmates. Despite the President's executive order and the testimony of our thought leaders and business leaders, we are not moving fast enough to curtail the continued damage this technology is doing and will do as it evolves. Not only has it been used for non-consensual pornography, cyberbullying, and harassment, causing great harm to individuals, but the potential for national security implications are grave. Deepfakes can be used to impersonate government officials, military personnel, or law enforcement, and, in general, lead to misinformation and potentially dangerous situations.

Today, this is no longer a problem that can be solved by simply detecting and removing generated content from our social media and content provider sites. I urge you to consider legislation and regulation to address the misuse of deepfake technology as a whole. Striking the right balance between free speech and safeguards to protect against malicious uses of deepfakes is essential. First and foremost, public awareness and digital literacy programs are vital to helping individuals learn about the existence of deepfakes and how to ensure that they do not propagate this type of misinformation. It may seem obvious that people want to know what type of information is being generated, and you would hope that they would be able to hold it upon themselves not to spread it, but we find that that is not the case. We should consider including school media literacy education and promote critical thinking. Collaboration between Congress and technology companies is essential, and I am glad to see that that is happening to address the challenges posed by deepfakes. Tech companies should be responsible for developing and implementing the policies to detect and mitigate this type of content, including what we were hearing today, on their platforms and sharing, most importantly, what they learn with others. We have addressed this type of a problem with our cybersecurity, and we should be doing that same thing with our misinformation. More robust privacy and consent laws are needed to protect individuals from using their likeness and voice in deepfake content without their permission, and continued research and development in AI deepfake technology are necessary, as is funding to counter deepfake misuse.

We have created these problems, but I have no doubt that if we work together, we are smart enough to figure out how to solve them. I look forward to taking your questions.

Ms. MACE. Thank you. I now recognize Mr. Gregory to please begin his opening statement.

Statement of Sam Gregory Executive Director Witness

Mr. GREGORY. Chairwoman Mace, Ranking Member Connolly, and Members of the Subcommittee, I am Sam Gregory, Executive Director of the human rights organization, WITNESS. Since 2018, WITNESS has led a global effort—Prepare, Don't Panic—to inclusively prepare for deepfake and related synthetic media and generative AI technologies. The capabilities and uses of deepfakes have often been overhyped, but with recent shifts, the moment to address them more comprehensively has come. First, I will cover technological advances.

Commercialization and accessibility characterized changes in the last year. Deepfake technologies are now available in widely used consumer tools, not just niche apps. Furthermore, they are easy to use and, particularly for audio and image, can be instructed with plain language and require no coding skills. Realistic image generation has improved dramatically in its quality and customization in a year. With widely available audio cloning tools, 1 minute of audio is enough to fake a voice. While video remains harder to do in complex real-world scenarios, consumer apps can swap an individual's face onto another's body, strip the clothing from a woman's body. Matching lip movements to a new audio track in a video is being demoed by Google, and live deepfakes are feasible. As a result, we are seeing an increased volume and ease in creating variations of realistic synthetic photos, audio, and, eventually, video of specific real individuals and contexts.

I would like to flag four future trends. These are increasing ease in instructing these tools in plain language; two, more ability to tailor outputs; three, more realistic outputs; and four, eventually similar advances in video to what we now see in audio and images. Moving on to the risks and harms, deepfakes are causing harms in the U.S. and globally, with disproportionate impacts on groups already at risk of discrimination or vulnerable to offline harms. Women and girls are widely targeted with nonconsensual sexual images, and this problem is escalating. AI-generated child sexual abuse material, CSAM, is increasing. Simulated audio scams are proliferating, as are misuses of AI audio in political contexts. My organization frequently sees claims of AI generation used to muddy the waters and dismiss critical real content, while actors and others have their likenesses stolen to use in non-satirical commercial contexts.

Political processes are likely to be impacted by deepfakes, and recent polls find the American public is fearful of their impact. However, it is unreasonable to expect individuals to spot deceptive, yet realistic, deepfake imagery and voices. Guidance to look for the six-fingered hand or inspect visual errors in a pope in a puffer jacket does not help in the long run. Meanwhile, under resourced newsrooms and community leaders across the political spectrum are under pressure and do not have access to reliable tools that can detect deepfakes. That is because deepfake detection efforts are not yet reliable at scale or across multiple different ways of creating deepfakes, nor are there widely shared methods to clearly indicate how AI was used in creating content.

This leads me to what Congress should consider, to address these advances in technology and accompanying misuses. First, enact Federal legislation around existing harms, including nonconsensual sexual content and the growing use of generative AI and CSAM. Incorporating broad consultation with groups working on these existing harms while safeguarding constitutional and human rights would help you craft appropriate steps. Second, since people will not be able to spot deepfake content with their eyes or ears, we need solutions to proactively add and show the provenance of AI content and, if desired and under certain circumstances, human-generated content. Provenance, such as the C2PA standard mentioned before, means showing people how content and communications were made, edited, and distributed, as well as other information that explains the recipe. The best choices here will go beyond binary ‘‘yes’’/‘‘no’’ labels.

Overall, these transparency approaches provide a signal of AI usage, but they do not, per se, indicate deception and must be accompanied by public education. Critically, these approaches should protect privacy and not collect, by default, personally identifiable information. For content that is not AI generated, we should be wary of how any provenance approach can be misused for surveillance and stifling freedom of speech.

My third recommendation is on detection. Alongside indicating how the content we consume was made, there is a continuing need for after-the-fact detection for content believed to be AI generated. From witnesses' experience, the skills and tools to detect AI-generated media remain unavailable to the people who need them the most, including journalists, rights defenders, and election officials domestically and globally. It remains critical to support Federal research and investment in this area to improve detection overall and to close this gap. It should be noted that both provenance and detection are not as relevant to nonconsensual sexual deepfakes where a real versus fake is often beside the point since the harm is caused in other ways. We need other responses to that.

As a general and final statement for both detection and provenance to be effective in helping the public to understand how deepfake technologies are used in the media we consume, we need a clear pipeline of responsibility that includes all the technology actors involved in the production of AI technologies more broadly, from the foundation models, to those designing and deploying software and apps, to the platforms that disseminate content. Thank you for the opportunity to testify.

Ms. MACE. Thank you. I will now recognize Mr. Overton to begin your opening statement.

Statement of Spencer Overton Professor of Law George Washington School of Law

Mr. OVERTON. Chairwoman Mace, Ranking Member Connolly, Subcommittee Members, thanks for inviting me to testify. My name is Spencer Overton. I am a professor at GW Law School and GW's Equity Institute. My research focuses on civil rights law, democracy, and disinformation.

Now, while deepfake technologies offer many benefits, they also threaten democratic values, and they produce harms disproportionately borne by women and communities of color. Nina Jankowitz, for example, is a 34-year-old researcher. She specializes in state-sponsored disinformation and gendered online abuse. Earlier this year, she found out she was featured in at least three synthetic videos that appear to show her engaging in sex acts. Now, she wrote about these videos.

She wrote, quote, and I will just use her words, ''Although they may provide cheap thrills for the viewer, their deeper purpose is to humiliate, shame, and objectify women, especially women who have the temerity to speak out. Users can also easily find deepfake porn videos of the singer, Taylor Swift; the actress Emma Watson; and the former Fox News host, Megyn Kelly. Democratic officials, such as Kamala Harris, Nancy Pelosi, Alexandria Ocasio-Cortez, and Republicans Nikki Haley and Elise Stefanik, and countless other prominent women. By simply existing as women in public life, we have all become targets, stripped of our accomplishments, our intellect, and our activism, and reduced to sex objects for the pleasure of millions of anonymous eyes.''

Deepfake pornography accounts for, as you all said, over 90 percent of all deepfake videos online. Women are featured as the primary subjects of 99 percent of deepfake pornography, while men are the primary subjects in only 1 percent. Nonconsensual deepfake pornography does not simply hurt women's feelings. It is an antidemocratic form of harassment designed to silence and undermine public confidence in women as legitimate public policy leaders. Deepfake technology is also fueling racial harassment. Earlier this year, a deepfake video showed a middle school principal saying that Black students should be sent back to Africa, calling them monkeys and the ''N'' word, and threatening gun violence. User-friendly and affordable, deepfake technology could allow bad actors to be even more effective in dividing Americans and undermining democracy.

So, when we think back to 2016, the Russians, we know, set up social media accounts pretending to be Black Americans. They posted calls for racial justice, developed a following, and then, just before Election Day, they targeted ads at Black users, encouraging them to boycott the election and not vote. Now today, in this world, the Russians or domestic bad actors could spark social upheaval by creating deepfake videos of a white police officer shooting an unarmed Black person. Indeed, earlier this year, just before Chicago's mayoral election, a deepfake video went viral of a candidate casually suggesting that regular police killings of civilians was normal, and that candidate lost. Now, the private sector is definitely important, but the market alone will not solve all of these problems. Initial studies, for example, show that deepfake detection systems have higher error rates for videos showing people of color.

In conclusion, as deepfake technology becomes more common, women and communities of color bear increasing burdens. Members of Congress should come together, understand these emerging challenges, and really take action to protect all Americans and our democracy from the harms. Thank you.

Ms. MACE. Thank you. I would now like to recognize myself for 5 minutes for questioning, and my first question is for every member of the panel. So, let us not do 5 minutes each because we only have 5 minutes today, so if you could just keep it brief.

I am very concerned about deepfake technology being weaponized against women and children. Mr. Overton, as you made your point, the overwhelming majority of deepfakes circulating are pornographic. Most of these involve images of women. Some are images of children. As a woman in a public position and the mother of a teenage daughter, it is alarming to me how easy it has become to create and distribute realistic pornographic images of actual women and girls. These images can cause lifelong and lasting humiliation and harm to that woman or girl. So, what can we do to protect women and children from being abused in this manner? Mr. Ibraham, and we will just go across the panel.

Mr. IBRAHIM. Thank you, Congresswoman. Indeed, this is, as everyone noted, the main issue right now with generative AI, and there are no immediate silver bullets. So, several colleagues have noted media literacy and education and awareness. Also, a lot of these nonconsensual pornographic images are made from open- source models. There are ways in which open-source models can potentially leverage things, like provenance and watermarking——

Ms. MACE. Mm-hmm.

Mr. IBRAHIM [continuing]. So that the outputs of those models will have those marks, and law enforcement can better detect, better trace down and take down such images. Those are just some thoughts to begin with.

Ms. MACE. Thank you. Mr. Doermann?

Mr. DOERMANN. One of the challenges that we have is that we do not have a culture where a lot of these things are unacceptable. In the case of New Jersey, I understand that there were parents even that said boys will be boys. These are not the kinds of things that we have today that should allow these types of things to progress from a technology point of view. We do have the ability to do partial image search. As another panelist here said, we have the original source material, and we could check that something has been manipulated in that way. It just requires that we do it at scale. It is not an easy solution, but those are the types of things that we have to think sort of outside the box.

Ms. MACE. Mr. Gregory? Microphone.

Mr. GREGORY. There is a patchwork of state laws at the moment. There is no Federal law at the moment that would protect women and girls. We need to make it clearer where there is individual liability that can be applied here. I should also note that recent research indicates how easy it is to find these deepfakes on search engines. Just type in a name plus ‘‘deepfakes,’’ and you will come up with a deepfake of a public figure. So, addressing the responsibility of platforms within to make sure that, it is less easy to do that because at the moment, it is very hard for individuals to chase down all the examples of their deepfakes online with individual requests.

Ms. MACE. Mr. Overton?

Mr. OVERTON. The proposed Preventing Deepfakes of Intimate Images Act is a good start. Having both criminal and civil penalties is important. Not having overly burdensome intent requirements to establish a violation and also focusing on both creators and distributors, those are some important factors.

Ms. MACE. Thank you. My next question is about laws. Do we need changes in law enforcement practice? And there are revenge porn laws, as an example, that do not cover deepfakes necessarily. On the Federal level, 15 U.S. Code, Section 6851—I happened to be reading about it today-is civil action related to intimate images and videos, but it relates to real images and videos, not to deepfakes. And so, I see a huge gap in law and even law enforcement practice, and what are your thoughts on that? Mm-hmm. We have a minute, so everybody gets, like, 20 seconds.

Mr. IBRAHIM. I would encourage examination of laws and what generative AI platforms and models can do——

Ms. MACE. Mm-hmm.

Mr. IBRAHIM [continuing]. To pre-mark their content output so that we can better effectively take things down and track them.

Mr. DOERMANN. I think I am not a legal scholar, but, you know, it is my understanding that, you know, the same way as our first generative algorithms targeted very high-level individuals, it might not be just pornographic. It might be just showing somebody in another type of compromising situation.

Ms. MACE. Mm-hmm.

Mr. DOERMANN. We need comprehensive laws to address these things.

Ms. MACE. Mr. Gregory.

Mr. GREGORY. Extending Federal law to cover synthetic content——

Ms. MACE. Mm-hmm.

Mr. GREGORY [continuing]. That fulfills the same purpose as a revenge porn and making sure it is accessible globally. We encounter cases of this all over the world.

Ms. MACE. Thank you. Mr. Overton?

Mr. OVERTON. Yes. I concur with Mr. Gregory.

Ms. MACE. That was easy. All right. Thank you, and I will yield for 5 minutes to my colleague, Mr. Connolly.

Mr. CONNOLLY. Thank you, Madam Chairwoman. You know, it seems to me that this is not as simple as it seems. Let us take AI for pornography. So, if somebody is a caricaturist and uses AI, and they want to make fun of a political figure and they make him to be the emperor with no clothes, crown on the head, and he is walking around with no clothes to make the point that he is empty, he is without merit or politically lost, now that is not pornography. It is AI-generative technology. It is not the real thing, but the parameters of the law, being a public official, you have got to put up with a fair amount. On the other hand, if somebody took that same individual and used it clearly as, not a caricature, not fun, but in a pornographic AI-generative technology, has he crossed a line in terms of the law, Professor Overton?

Mr. OVERTON. So, I think the answer is yes. Obviously, we have got to be very sensitive in terms of these First Amendment issues, including satire and parody, that type of thing. I would say, though, that even if we have disclosure in terms of deepfakes, this targeting of women who are political figures, even if it is satire, I think that it is a problem and something that we really need to hone in on.

Mr. CONNOLLY. I agree with you, but you are the professor of law, not me. Surely you appreciate the delicacy of that——

Mr. OVERTON. Right.

Mr. CONNOLLY [continuing]. However, under our constitutional system.

Mr. OVERTON. Correct.

Mr. CONNOLLY. We have limits for public officials to be able to seek redress in terms of libel.

Mr. OVERTON. That is right.

Mr. DOERMANN. You can defame us——

Mr. OVERTON. New York Times v. Sullivan.

Mr. CONNOLLY. Yes. You can defame us in a way you cannot defame some other citizens, New York Times v. Sullivan, so we have high standards for public officials.

Mr. OVERTON. Yes.

Mr. CONNOLLY. So, I put that as a category of complexity.

Mr. OVERTON. Right.

Mr. CONNOLLY. Not so simple in terms of regulating.

Mr. OVERTON. It is something we have got to grapple with. I really refer you to Mary Anne Franks, my colleague at GW, did a great Law Review article in 2019 where she really chronicled these harms as not really contributing to free speech and the marketplace of ideas and truth. And so, there is something else that is here, and we have got to really grapple with it.

Mr. CONNOLLY. Right. I agree with you. I do not think it is as simple—

Mr. OVERTON. Right.

Mr. CONNOLLY [continuing]. As we would all like.

Mr. OVERTON. Yep.

Mr. CONNOLLY. Now, that is public officials.

Mr. OVERTON. Mm-hmm.

Mr. CONNOLLY. Private individuals, such as the girls we talked about in New Jersey, are pure victims of somebody else's perverse sense of fun or pleasure, and they suffer real harm. Legally, what is their protection? What is their redress right now?

Mr. OVERTON. Yes. Right now, the problem is a lot of law does not cover this, and some states have laws with regard to deepfakes, but many states do not. Even though almost all states have revenge porn laws, this activity does not clearly fall under that, so often, there is no recourse.

Mr. CONNOLLY. So, we could maybe use the sort of underage piece of law to get at this if these victims are under a certain age.

Mr. OVERTON. I think that that is correct, but even the CSAM issue that we talked about before is not always clearly covered here in terms of existing laws with regard to child pornography. So, you know, we have got some real holes in the law.

Mr. CONNOLLY. Yes. OK. Well, I think that is really worthy of an explanation, not only by us up here, but by your profession and by the academic community. Dr. Doermann, let us send you back in time. You are back at DARPA, and you are in charge of all AI research and projects. What are we not doing that you want to see funded? You know, pick two or three that we really ought to be doing right now because it could have a beneficial effect if we plow this ground in terms of its promise in protecting ourselves from deepfakes.

Mr. DOERMANN. Absolutely. It is not just deepfakes, you are right. It is AI in general. We have gotten to the point where these large language models, where these models that we have are completely unexplainable. People believe that AI is somehow an answer, and everything is always right that comes out of these systems. We cannot converse with these systems, and they cannot explain why they made a decision or how they made things, I think the explainability issues. And these are things that DARPA is looking at now, but we need to have the trust and the safety aspects explored at the grassroots level for all of these things.

Mr. CONNOLLY. I would just say, Madam Chair, my time is up, but I think there is a huge difference between the pope in a puffery jacket, which does not do much harm, and the example of Ukraine, where deepfakes has him saying we are putting down our arms and surrendering. You know, that can cause or end a conflict in an undesirable way, and so clearly protecting ourselves and being able to counter that disinformation in a very expeditious way, if not preventing it to begin with, I think is kind of the goal. I thank you.

Ms. MACE. Thank you, Mr. Connolly. I now recognize Mr. Timmons for 5 minutes.

Mr. TIMMONS. Thank you, Madam Chair. It seems we have two main issues here. One is attribution—a lot of people would see a deepfake video and not know whether it was fake or real—and the next issue is updating our legal structures to address the core purpose of them. We have revenge porn laws in many states. The update to the Violence Against Women Act that Chairwoman Mace just mentioned gives a civil cause of action for $150,000. The purpose of that was to address this issue, and the legislative intent did not really keep in mind the possibility of a deepfake. If you cannot distinguish it, there is no difference.

So, I guess my first question, Dr. Doermann, is there any way that we can, one, mandate identification to show that it is an altered image or a fake image, and then, two, is there a way to mandate that in the Code? Just like a photo on my iPhone says where it is and the GPS location it was taken, could you do the same thing with an IP address, and a location, and a time, and a date stamp on the video, and mandate that and make it illegal to create images using this technology without the attribution component? Does my question make sense?

Mr. DOERMANN. Yes. I think you actually have two parts there. Well, first of all, you know, if you mandate creating content or creating things that require you to disclose, for example, that it is a deepfake, the adversaries and the people that are doing these bad things in the first place, they are not going to follow those rules anyway. I mean, that is a much lower bar than actually creating pornographic images.

Mr. TIMMONS. Well, we got to take the first step of U.S. citizens within our jurisdiction.

Mr. DOERMANN. We can, yes.

Mr. TIMMONS. So, I mean, we could easily say if you create this, there is a civil penalty that is available, and that if you do this, there is a criminal penalty, just like states have done with revenge porn.

Mr. DOERMANN. Again, there is also a continuum between the things that are used for good and the things that it is used for bad, so just saying that you are going to, you know, identify it.

Mr. TIMMONS. OK. Deepfake porn, we could literally use AI to say whether something is considered porn or not and then whether that is——

Mr. DOERMANN. I am not sure about that. I think we will have a continuum of these——

Mr. TIMMONS. Well, you are going to have to take a photo of somebody initially of their face or their likeness to then give the AI the ability to create something that is resembling the original human, and you could then——

Mr. DOERMANN. Well, the face is, but the original content can come from a legal pornographic film, for example, and that is what is happening.

Mr. TIMMONS. But you are putting someone's face on it that is not the same face——

Mr. DOERMANN. That is——

Mr. TIMMONS [continuing]. To make it look like them in an attempt to do the same thing that we have revenge porn laws to do.

Mr. DOERMANN. That is what my colleagues here are saying, that there are holes in these laws that do not necessarily allow you to do that, those——

Mr. TIMMONS. Mr. Overton, is there any argument that you could use the existing statute to file a Federal lawsuit against somebody for sharing a deepfake?

Mr. OVERTON. There is an argument. I think the question is, does it hold water.

Mr. TIMMONS. We have got some judges in this country that do just about anything. All right.

Mr. OVERTON. Right, but, you know, we want certainly some consistency in enforcement of law.

Mr. TIMMONS. Sure. We could also maybe expand the Code se tion, too, but, I mean, I guess then it becomes the whole purpose of revenge porn law is, theoretically, you were complicit in the initial video but not complicit in the sharing, and it has to be done for retribution of some kind. So, I guess it becomes a lot more complicated when you are talking about celebrities and whatnot, but they also deserve the same degree of privacy and respect that we are seeking for everyone else. OK. Let us go back. I mean, I——

Mr. OVERTON. Well, let me just followup here. Disclosure under the court is much more acceptable than complete restrictions here, you know, in terms of the First Amendment.

Mr. TIMMONS. OK. And I guess, Dr. Doermann, back to the attribution issue. I mean, it is not unreasonable to try to create a legal framework through which a photo that is taken on my iPhone has all of this metadata. I mean, theoretically, if that metadata is not present in a video, then we would know that it is a malicious and does that——

Mr. DOERMANN. Yes. Yes. In theory, yes. The problem comes, again, with enforcing this because you now are forcing individuals to mark their content. It is a——

Mr. TIMMONS. Could we use AI to seek out and automatically delete videos that do not have the——

Mr. DOERMANN. Absolutely, and you could forge this type of stuff as well. Even camera fingerprints, these things can be forged, so we just have to be careful about what we rely on, and we make sure that everybody is playing by the same rules in being able to enforce those types of things.

Mr. TIMMONS. Theoretically, we could mandate certain websites to use AI to identify deepfakes and automatically delete them if they are deemed pornographic. Theoretically.

Mr. DOERMANN. Theoretically.

Mr. TIMMONS. OK. All right. Sorry, Madam Chair. Thank you. I yield back.

Ms. MACE. No. Thank you. I will now recognize Mr. Burchett for 5 minutes.

Mr. BURCHETT. Thank you, Chairlady. Several questions. I am just going to ramble, if it is all right with you all. This is a question to all of you all, and I would like to discuss how criminals are using this deepfake technology to produce child sex abuse material, just child porn. And when these criminals use this deepfake technology to make this material of children, rather than alter the images that already exist, how can law enforcement agencies determine the age of the subject in the material?

Mr. IBRAHIM. Yes, sir. We have seen a rising amount of cases. The New Jersey one was noted. There was also a recent case in Spain in which these models were used for underage young girls. In terms of how can law enforcement potentially use that information and detect, there is some growing thinking that if the models themselves add some watermark or provenance to everything——

Mr. BURCHETT. And explain to me the watermark. What is that?

Mr. IBRAHIM. So, it——

Mr. BURCHETT. I know what it means, but maybe explain it.

Mr. IBRAHIM. It would be an invisible algorithm that is attached to every image that is spit out of the generator, whether it is a benign or malicious image, and which could be decoded by a law enforcement agency or has some sort of chain of custody, that could potentially be useful. That is something that a variety of organizations are looking at.

Mr. BURCHETT. All right.

Mr. DOERMANN. We also have to educate our legal system on how to use these things. I was on a panel at AAAS about a month ago, and very simple things such as the use of face recognition as an AI tool, which we know has been controversial, to say the least. So, we just have to make sure that our content providers or service providers are on board and that they are sharing this type of information with each other, and that is definitely something that is doable.

Mr. GREGORY. The problem this is creating in CSAM has similarities to other problems. It is a volume problem where you then have a triage problem for the people who have to do the investigation because of creating synthesized images and adapting existing images. So, investing in tools that are available to law enforcement as well as others who have to do that triage work would be a critical next step.

Mr. OVERTON. I just would note these evidentiary issues are very challenging for law enforcement.

Mr. BURCHETT. Yes. I think the court cases are that if they just generate, like, a fake face, that they cannot be held for child porn. Is that correct?

Mr. DOERMANN. It is my understanding that those laws are changing, but the previous laws—again, I am not a legal scholar— required a victim, and that was really the loophole there.

Mr. BURCHETT. Yes.

Mr. DOERMANN. But they are closing those.

Mr. BURCHETT. OK. Well, how can we prevent this technology from being used to create child sex abuse material? Mr. Overton, we will start with you first, brother.

Mr. OVERTON. I think that legislation is very important that directly deals with the CSAM issue.

Mr. GREGORY. I will agree with Mr. Overton. It is legislation around CSAM. There are clear reasons to legislate and include this alongside non-synthetic images.

Mr. DOERMANN. And I will just emphasize from the technology point of view, this is a genie that is out of the bottle. We are not going to put it back in.

Mr. BURCHETT. Yes.

Mr. DOERMANN. These types of technologies are out there. They could use it on adults, consenting adults, the same way, and it is going to be difficult to legislate those, but the technology is there. It is on the laptops of anyone that wants to download it from the internet, and so the legislation part is the best approach.

Mr. IBRAHIM. I echo my colleagues, and I would just note the majority of these materials are often done through open-source models. So, the more models you can get to sign up to frameworks and guardrails, pushing bad actors into other models that are harder to use would be beneficial.

Mr. BURCHETT. Do you all agree that these AI-generated images of children, real or not, should be illegal?

Mr. IBRAHIM. I do.

Mr. DOERMANN. Absolutely. Mr. GREGORY. Yes.

Mr. OVERTON. Yes. We assume they are not hurting children. They are, yes.

Mr. BURCHETT. Yes. You know, I sponsored some legislation in Tennessee where actually people that abused children were given the death penalty, and my statement was that they had given these kids a lifetime sentence, and there is no coming back from that. It is a lifetime of guilt, and you see a lot of the kids self-inflict wounds and take their own lives, and it is just brutal. So anyway, thank you all. Chairlady?

Ms. MACE. Yes, thank you. I will now recognize Mr. Burlison for 5 minutes.

Mr. BURLISON. Thank you. I will begin with Mr. Doermann. Can we talk about the technology that is possibly available to recognize or identify AI and how that might be applied in a commercial setting?

Mr. DOERMANN. Well, the biggest challenge of any of these technologies is the scale. Even if you have an algorithm that works at 99.9 percent, the amount of data that we have at scale that run through our major service providers makes the false alarm rates almost prohibitive. We need to have a business model that our service providers, our content providers have that makes them want to take these things down. If they get clicks, that is what is selling ads now, and if it is not illegal, if we cannot hold them responsible in any way, it makes it very difficult to convince them to do anything.

Mr. BURLISON. Given that currently, today, there is the ability to identify graphic content, violent content, and then to often block it or require a person to take some action to basically break the glass and go through and see that content, can that not be applied to deepfake images or things that are created with it? That way, the individual would at least know that there is no truth to this image.

Mr. DOERMANN. Absolutely, I mean, but the places that this content is showing up are on those pay sites or onsites where it is mixed in with other type of content, so just detecting it is not necessarily the issue.

Mr. BURLISON. And they do not have a self-interest, a financial interest in identifying the deepfakes.

Mr. DOERMANN. Correct.

Mr. BURLISON. OK. I understand what you are saying. So let me ask, the technology is capable. We just need to identify——

Mr. DOERMANN. Not necessarily the deepfake part. If you do a reverse image search, for example, in a number of different sites, you can do it for the entire image, but if you take just the face of an individual, that is what we really need. We need to be able to say, OK, we are not going to look at the entire video because this video is not real, right? Well, part of it is real. The video part of the nude body is real, and the face is generated. So, if we could identify those people, make sure that we have that consent before it gets spread, that might be one thing, but, you know, just to detect something as being pornographic, we are still not detecting the fact that it was generated with a fake.

Mr. BURLISON. The deepfake. You are saying that there is technology, AI, that can view videos and images and ascertain whether it is a deepfake?

Mr. DOERMANN. Not reliably enough.

Mr. BURLISON. There currently is not any.

Mr. DOERMANN. This is 85 percent maybe, and every time we release a tool that detects this, our adversaries can use AI to cover up that trace evidence. So, no, that is why I said in my opening statement that detection and trying to pull this stuff down is no longer a solution. We need to have a much bigger solution.

Mr. BURLISON. Mr. Gregory, how do we authenticate the content without creating a surveillance state or suppressing free expression?

Mr. GREGORY. The first thing I would say is, as we are looking at authenticity and provenance measures, ways that you can show how something was made with AI and perhaps with human inputs, and I think we should recognize that the future of media production is complex. It will not just be a yes or no of AI. It will be, yes, AI was used here, no, AI was not, here is a human. So, it is really important that we actually focus this on the how media was made, not the who, right? So, you should know, for example, that a piece of media was made with an AI tool, was altered perhaps to change an element of it, and that might be the critical information rather than a political satirist made this piece of media, which, you know, certainly would not be something we would want to see here in the U.S. and globally when you look at how that could be misused.

So, I think we are entering a complicated scenario where it is both the authenticity tools and also detection tools, my experience, of a very messy reality where we need to focus on both, but we have got to do it with civil liberties and privacy at heart.

Mr. BURLISON. OK. As I understand it, there is—and this is a question for Mr. Ibrahim. What is the difference between detecting deepfakes and content authentication?

Mr. IBRAHIM. Detecting deepfakes would be something you do after the fact. It would be a system that would look at a video and try to spit out a binary or results-based response. Content authentication or provenance does it while it is being created. That is what Truepic does. So, as the image is being captured from a phone or a smartphone or a piece of hardware, you are attaching and cryptographically hashing the time, the date, the location, et cetera, into the media file while it is being created, so it is a proactive measure versus a reactive measure.

Mr. BURLISON. My time has expired.

Ms. MACE. Thank you. I want to thank all of our witnesses for being here today. In closing, I want to thank you for your testimony again.

So, with that, and without objection, all Members will have 5 legislative of days within which to submit materials and to submit additional written questions for the witnesses, which will be forwarded to the witnesses for their response.

Ms. MACE. So, if there is no further business, without objection, the Subcommittee stands adjourned.

[Whereupon, at 4:43 p.m., the Subcommittee was adjourned.]

Chapter 2

Addressing Real Harm Done by Deepfakes*

Committee on Oversight and Accountability

Tuesday, March 12, 2024

U.S. House of Representatives
Committee on Oversight and Accountability
Subcommittee on Cybersecurity, Information Technology,
and Government Innovation
Washington, D.C.

The Subcommittee met, pursuant to notice, at 2:27 p.m., in room 2154, Rayburn House Office Building, Hon. Nancy Mace [Chairwoman of the Subcommittee] presiding.

Present: Representatives Mace, Timmons, Burchett, Luna, Langworthy, Connolly, Lynch, and Pressley.

Also present: Representatives Raskin, Garcia, and Morelle.

Ms. MACE. The Subcommittee on Cybersecurity, Information Technology, and Government Innovation will now come to order, and we welcome everyone who is here this afternoon.

Without objection, the Chair may declare a recess at any time. And I do want to ask for unanimous consent at this time for Representative Morelle from New York to be waived on to the Subcommittee for today's hearing for the purposes of asking questions.

So, without objection, so ordered.

---

* This is an edited, reformatted and augmented version of Hearing Before the Subcommittee on Cybersecurity, Information Technology, and Government Innovation of the Committee on Oversight and Accountability, U.S. House of Representatives, One Hundred Eighteenth Congress, Second Session, Serial No. 118–94, dated March 12, 2024.

In: The Deepfake Dilemma
Editor: Ruben Faulkner
ISBN: 979-8-90134-122-3

And thank you for being here today, and we have a few extra Members that will come in as well this afternoon.

I would like to recognize myself for the purpose of making an opening statement.

First of all, I want to say thank you to all of our witnesses who are here today. AI deepfakes, nonconsensual photos/photography are only getting worse in this country and around the world because of the advent of technology, and we are very eager to hear from each and every one of you today. If you did not get a chance to watch ABC "This Week" on Sunday and see the way George Stephanopoulos handled the topic of rape, I would encourage everyone watching this today to go and watch it.

I have been working on women's issues for a very long time. The body of work that I have been working on is only becoming more extensive because of the advent of technology. I wanted to point out today for my constituents back home some of the legislation that I have been working on. For example, H.R. 5721, has to do with rape. Rape is an issue that I care about, near and dear to my heart. I do not believe in rape shaming rape victims, but I did a bill that would work on the backlog for rape kits in this country.

There are over 100,000 rape kits that are sitting on shelves today that law enforcement have not processed, and I want women to know here today and in the hearing, those that are watching, those around the country, to know that Congress cares. We care about victims of sexual crimes.

And another bill, most recently, there was a decision in Alabama about IVF, and I have sponsored a resolution, I guess 2 weeks ago, House Resolution 1043, that talks about IVF and my desire to make sure that we, one, condemn the Alabama ruling, but two, also we do everything we can to protect women and their access to IVF. And it is not just a women's issue. It is a family issue. It is men and women alike who want to start a family. And both sides of the aisle, I know that we both want to work to make sure that we protect women and men and their access to reproductive technology and the ability to have a family.

I recently rolled out last week a deepfake bill, an initiative that would take a look at it from a criminal perspective. You know, we have a lot of laws in this country. Some states talk about revenge porn. Some have, you know, obviously, peeping Tom laws, surreptitious recording laws, but really, the advent of deepfakes and technology and AI is really a new frontier, and we will hear from you all today about this. But I filed a bill with some of my colleagues last week that would take deepfakes, if they are in the likeness of a real person, and make it a crime. This is not a crime yet today, and when the

FBI or when you are looking to charge someone or indict someone for criminal behavior, it has got to be under Title 18. So, we looked at Chapter 88, Title 18 of the Federal Code of laws and looked at how we can make it a crime. I also recently cosponsored a bill by Alexandria Ocasio-Cortez on deepfakes, but it was related to civil torts.

I have learned a lot in the last hundred days or so, due to some experiences that I have recently had, about our Nation's laws and how poor they are on nonconsensual recordings of people, whether they are real or whether they are deepfakes. I am going to be introducing a bill next week, I believe, on voyeurism, again, looking at Title 18. When the Violence against Women Act was done, there was a civil tort enabled for women who are victims of voyeurism at the Federal level, but there was no crime. Like, it is not a crime to do that at the Federal level, and I am, you know, sort of astonished that there is not. But those are just a smattering of things that I have been working on up here in Congress.

I did want to enter into the record this afternoon and wanted to ask unanimous consent to enter into the record two articles. One is out of People magazine. State House Rep. Brandon Guffey, his son committed suicide. His son was 17. The title of the article is, ''His Son, 17, Was a Sextortion Victim, Then Died by Suicide. Now South Carolina Dad Protects Other Kids From the Same Fate.'' This is difficult for me to read, but Brandon Guffey was typing on his phone at his home in Rock Hill, South Carolina. All of a sudden, he heard a sound. It sounded like a bowling ball falling and crashing through shelves, Brandon told People magazine. He yelled for his son, Gavin Guffey, who was in the bathroom with the door locked. When the 17-year-old failed to answer, Brandon kicked in the door and found his oldest child lying on the floor bleeding. He thought that he fell and hit his head. After the shouting from his wife, they called 9–1–1. Brandon said he could smell the gun and the taste of gunpowder.

Brandon's son committed suicide because of being shamed and blackmailed over photographs on Meta, on social media, and it is very hard for me as a mom to hear these stories that have had kids affected by online scammers on social media. But it gets worse because with the advent of deepfakes and AI and technology, it is not just real videos you have to be worried about. It is the fake ones now that can be easily created.

The second article I wanted to ask unanimous consent to be entered into the record is a recent article in the Post and Courier and the title of it is, ''Member of Aiken Winter Colony Family Still Facing Voyeurism Charges.'' This guy had a hidden camera in an Airbnb, I guess, and under South Carolina

State Law Section 16– 17–470, where it is illegal to record anybody, this first-offense voyeurism is a misdemeanor. It is only a misdemeanor. The fine is $500, and you face only up to 3 years in jail. This guy, I believe, allegedly had thousands of videos of unsuspecting victims.

And recently and disturbingly, I learned of a real incident in my district where multiple women appeared to be recorded without their knowledge or their consent, over a dozen women in my district. And disturbingly, included in these videos and these photographs, that I have been made aware of, included sexual assault. As a rape victim, to learn about these things is deeply, deeply disturbing.

And as I just mentioned, these are the real stories of real women that are victims, but it is worse because with the advent of deepfakes and AI and technology, it is not the real videos. I mean, obviously we are worried about that, but now it can be created out of thin air, and that fake videos of real people are out there. We are going to hear your stories today, and some of you, I hope, will touch on legislative options, how do states address this, how does the Federal Government address this, how do we take care of this criminally, how do we take care of this civilly? Because women who are victims of such a disturbing thing, whether it is real or fake or deepfake, they ought to get justice in this country at the Federal and the state level. With AI technology moving forward very fast, here in this Subcommittee today, we are going to talk about this from policymakers and people and family and moms who have experienced this horrific thing called deepfake. We are going to hear about child pornography, something I cannot even talk about, what is happening in the deepfake and AI world with child porn. It is all deeply disturbing, and I look forward to hearing everyone's testimony today and how do we move forward from here and make sure that everyone who has been a victim has their voices heard and that they get justice when this happens.

Thank you, and I yield back to my colleague from Virginia, Mr. Connolly.

Mr. CONNOLLY. Thank you. Acknowledging the importance of this hearing during Women's History Month, I am grateful that we are gathered here today to highlight a sensitive but very deeply troubling subject. A 2023 study found that while 98 percent of all online deepfake videos were pornographic, women were the subjects in 99 percent of them. Our hope is that today's discussion will underscore the need for policy solutions that end the production, proliferation, and distribution of malicious deepfakes.

Earlier this year, artificial intelligence generated pornographic images of American pop star Taylor Swift rapidly spread on social media. Formerly known as Twitter, X, that platform and that company, proved very slow to act, and the images received, as a result, more than 47 million views in a matter of hours before X finally got around to removing them. Despite the images' removal, the explicit defects of the singer remain elsewhere online, and no laws exist to stop other malicious actors from reposting that material again. The fact that Ms. Swift, a globally recognized icon who built a $1 billion empire, cannot remove all nonconsensual deepfakes of herself, emphasizes that no one is safe.

Deplorably, children have also become victims of deepfake pornography. Last December, the Stanford Internet Observatory published an investigation that identified hundreds of images of child sexual abuse material, also known as CSAM, in an open data set that AI developers use to train popular AI text-to-image generation models. While methods exist to minimize CSAM in such data sets, it remains challenging to completely clean or stop the distribution of open data sets as the data are gathered by automated systems from a broad cross-section of the web, and they lack a central authority or host. Therefore, tech companies, leaders, victims, advertisers, and policymakers must come together to build a solution and address the issue head on.

Mrs. Dorata Mani, thank you for coming here today and bravely sharing your family's story. You and your daughter, Francesca, have proven to be fierce advocates against the creation and proliferation of nonconsensual deepfake pornography. You are providing a stalwart voice for countless others victimized by AI-generated deepfakes. I know President Biden has heard your heartfelt request for help because during his State of the Union address just this last week, he explicitly called upon Congress to better protect our children online in the new age of AI.

I also want to thank my multiple Democratic colleagues who requested to waive onto the Subcommittee today to speak out against harmful deepfakes. One of those Members, Representative Morelle, introduced the Preventing Deepfakes of Intimate Images Act, which would prohibit the creation and dissemination of nonconsensual defects of intimate images. As a cosponsor of this bill, I see that legislation as a great first step to preventing future wrongs that echo the fight of your family, Mrs. Mani.

Recent technological advancements in artificial intelligence have opened the door for bad actors with very little technical knowledge to create deepfakes cheaply and easily. Deepfake perpetrators can simply download apps that undress a person or swap their face onto nude images. That is why, if we want to keep up with the rapid proliferation of deepfakes, we must support Federal research and development of new tools for the detection and elimination of deepfake content. In addition, digital media literacy programs, which educate the public about deepfakes, have demonstrated effectiveness in vesting individuals with skills to critically evaluate content they consume online.

But we cannot have a fulsome discussion without acknowledging that some of our colleagues, including Members of this very Committee, have actively worked against rooting out the creation and dissemination of deepfakes. This Congress, the House Judiciary Committee Select Committee on Weaponization of the Federal Government, has relentlessly targeted government agencies, nonprofits, and academic researchers who are on the front line of this very work. These Members have stifled efforts of individuals and advocacy organizations actively trying to combat deepfakes and disinformation. For example, the Select Subcommittee accused the Federal Cybersecurity and Infrastructure Security Agency, CISA, of "colluding with Big Tech to censor certain viewpoints." These members argued that CISA's work to ensure election integrity, which, in part, includes defending against deepfake threats, is censorship.

They have also attempted to undermine the National Science Foundation's efforts to research manipulated and synthesized media and develop new technologies to detect. Most recently, on February 26, Chairman Jordan subpoenaed the NSF for documents and information regarding its research projects to prevent and detect deepfakes and other inauthentic information sources. He issued this subpoena even though the directive originated from a 2019 Republican championed law. Chairman Jordan has also targeted many of the academic researchers across the country who provide valuable research findings to the public and policymakers, such as the Stanford Internet Observatory, which led the investigation into CSAM's very questionable inclusion in AI training data sets.

I am proud of the Biden-Harris Administration secured voluntary commitments from seven major tech companies promising to work together with us and with government to ensure AI technologies are developed responsibly, but we know our work is not done. I urge my colleagues on both sides of the aisle to set aside partisan fishing expeditions and redirect our focus toward crafting bipartisan solutions to stop the creation of and dissemination of harmful deepfakes. I look forward to the hearing today, and I yield back.

Ms. MACE. Thank you. I am pleased now to introduce our witnesses for today's hearing. Our first witness is Mrs. Dorata Mani, a mother whose high school daughter was a victim of deepfake technology. We appreciate you being here today, Ms. Mani, to share your and your daughter's experience and message with us. Our second witness is Mr. John Shehan, Senior Vice President of the Exploited Children Division and International Engagement at the National Center for Missing and Exploited Children. Our third witness is Mr. Carl Szabo, Vice President and General Counsel of Netchoice, and our fourth witness today is Dr. Ari Ezra Waldman, professor of law at the University of California's Irvine School of Law. We welcome to have you and pleased to have you all here this afternoon.

Pursuant to Committee Rule 9(g), the witnesses will please stand and raise your right hands.

Do you solemnly swear or affirm that the testimony you are about to give is the truth, the whole truth, and nothing but the truth, so help you God?

[A chorus of ayes.]

Ms. MACE. Let the record show the witnesses answered in the affirmative.

We appreciate all of you being here today and look forward to your testimony. Let me remind the witnesses that we have read your written statements, and they will appear in full in the hearing record. Please limit your oral arguments to 5 minutes. As a reminder, please press the button on the microphone in front of you so that it is on, and Members up here can hear you. When you begin to speak, the light in front of you will turn green. After 4 minutes, the light will turn yellow. When the red light comes on, your 5 minutes has expired, and we are going to ask you to wrap up, and I will use the gavel nicely.

So, now I would like to recognize Mrs. Mani to please begin her opening statement.

Statement of Dorata Mani
Parent of Westfield (NJ) High School Student

Ms. MANI. Thank you so much for having me here. On October 20, 2023, a deeply troubling incident occurred involving my daughter and the Westfield High School administration and its students. It was confirmed that my daughter was one of several victims involved in the creation and distribution of AI deepfake nudes by her classmates. This event left her feeling helpless and powerless, intensified by the lack of accountability for the boys involved and the absence of protective laws, AI school policies, or even adherence to the school's own code of conduct and cyber harassment policies. Since that day, my daughter and I have been tirelessly advocating for the establishment of AI laws, the implementation of AI school policies, and the promotion of education regarding AI.

Despite being told repeatedly that nothing could be done, we find ourselves addressing this esteemed Committee today, highlighting the urgency and significance of this issue. Our advocacy has brought to light similar incidents from individuals across the globe, including Texas, D.C., Washington, Wisconsin, Australia, London, Japan, Germany, Greece, Spain, Paris, and more, indicating a widespread and pressing concern. We have identified several loopholes in the handling of AI-related incidents that demand attention from government bodies, educational institutions, and the media. However, our greatest disappointment lies in the school's handling of the situation, which we believe is indicative of a broader issue across all schools, given the ease and allure of creating AI-generated content.

Here, I wish to outline the mishandling of the situation by Westfield High School. One, the school inappropriately announced the names of the female AI victims over the intercom, compromising their privacy. The boys responsible for creating the nude photos were discreetly removed from the classroom, their identities protected. Only one boy was called over the intercom. When my daughter sought the support of a counselor during a meeting with the vice principal who was questioning her, her request was denied. The administration claimed the AI photographs were deleted without having seen them, offering no proof of their deletion. My attempts to communicate with the administration about the case have been constantly ignored.

A harassment, intimidation, and bullying report submitted in November 2023 has yet to yield a conclusive outcome which we should receive within 10 days of submission. The interviews, carried out at the school with underage suspects in the presence of police but without their parents, have made their statements inadmissible in court. Despite our submission of updated policies created by our lawyers at McCarter & English to the Westfield Board of Education, the school's cyber harassment policies and code of conduct remained outdated, referencing Walkmans, pagers, and beepers, with no mention of AI to this day. The school's communication focused on only one boy involved, ignoring the others. The accountability imposed for creating the AI deepfake nudes without girls' consent was a mere 1-day suspension for only one boy. This incident and the school's response underscores the urgent need for updated policies and a more responsible approach to handling AI-generated content and cyber harassment at schools.

In light of the recent incident at Beverly Hills Middle School from this month, Superintendent Bregy not only released a statement that the school's investigation is nearly completed 1 week after the incident, but also took crucial steps of contacting Congress to emphasize the urgency of prioritizing the safety of children in the United States, and today, I have learned from The Guardian that he expelled five students.

This proactive stance demonstrates a commendable commitment to facing uncomfortable truths head on, with a focus on educating and advocating for essential changes in how such incidents are handled. In contrast, my expectations for similar leadership and responsiveness from the principal at Westfield High School, Ms. Asfendis, have been met with disappointment. Given that the principal, like myself, is both a mother and an educator, I had hoped for a stronger stance in defending and supporting the girls at Westfield High School. Instead, there appears to be an effort to minimize the issue, hoping it will simply pass and fade away. This approach is not only disheartening, but also dangerous as it fosters an environment where female students are left to feel victimized while male students escape necessary accountability.

The discrepancy in handling such serious issues between schools like Beverly Hills and Westfield High is alarming and calls for immediate reevaluation and action to ensure all students are protected and supported equally in United States' schools.

Ms. MACE. Thank you. I now recognize Mr. Shehan for his opening statement.

Statement of John Shehan
Senior Vice President, Exploited Children Division & International Engagement
National Center for Missing and Exploited Children

Mr. SHEHAN. Good afternoon, Chairwoman Mace, Ranking Member Connolly, and the Members of the Subcommittee. My name is John Shehan, and I am a Senior Vice President at the National Center for Missing and Exploited Children, also known as NCMEC.

NCMEC is a private, nonprofit organization created in 1984. Our mission is to help reunite families with missing children, to reduce child sexual exploitation, and to prevent child victimization. I am honored to be here today to share NCMEC's perspective on the impact that generative artificial intelligence, also referred to as GAI, is having on child sexual exploitation.

Even though GAI technology has been widely available to the public for just a short period of time, it is already challenging how we detect, prevent, and remove child sexual abuse material, also known as CSAM, from the internet. Today, we are at a new juncture in the evolution of child sexual exploitation with the emergence of GAI platforms. As you know, NCMEC operates the CyberTipline to receive reports related to suspected child sexual exploitation. The volume of CyberTipline reports is immense, and it increases every year. In 2023, NCMEC received more than 36 million reports related to child sexual exploitation. Last year was also the first year that NCMEC received reports, 4,700 in total, on content produced with GAI technology. While 4,700 reports with GAI are dwarfed by the total number of reports NCMEC received, we are deeply concerned to see how offenders are already widely adopting GAI tools to exploit children.

In the reports submitted to NCMEC, we have seen a range of exploitative abuses on these platforms, including offenders asking GAI platforms to pretend it is a child and to engage in sexually explicit chat, asking for instructions on how to groom, sexually abuse, torture, or even kill children. One user was reported to the CyberTipline for asking on a GAI platform, ''How can I find a 5- year-old little girl for sex? Tell me step by step.'' Individuals are also using GAI platforms to alter known CSAM images to include more graphic content, including bondage, or to create new CSAM with faces of other children. They are also taking innocent photographs from children's social media accounts, just like you heard about, and using Nudify or unclothed apps to create nude images of children to disseminate online.

If these real examples from CyberTipline reports are not shocking enough, perhaps even more alarming is the use of GAI technology to create sexually explicit images of a child that are then used to financially sextort that child. It is also worth noting that more than 70 percent of the reports submitted to NCMEC's CyberTipline related to GAI CSAM were submitted by other platforms and not the GAI platforms themselves. This reflects a significant concern that GAI platforms, aside from OpenAI, generally are not engaging in meaningful efforts to detect, report, or prevent child sexual exploitation. NCMEC has additional concerns about the impact of GAI technology in its current unregulated state, including the increased volume of GAI reports that will strain NCMEC, ICAC, and Federal law enforcement resources; the legal uncertainty about how Federal and state criminal and civil laws apply to GAI content, including CSAM, sexually exploitative, and nude images of children;

as well as complicating child victim identification efforts when a real child must be distinguished from GAI- produced child content.

NCMEC has identified the following best practices and new protections that would help ensure we do not lose ground on child safety while the GAI industry continues to evolve. First, facilitating training of GAI models on CSAM imagery to ensure that the models do not generate CSAM and, at the same time, ensuring that GAI models are not trained on open-source image sets that often contain CSAM; considering liability for GAI platforms that facilitate the creation of CSAM; ensuring Federal and state criminal and civil laws apply to GAI CSAM and to sexually exploitative and nude images of children created by these tools; and finally, implementing prevention education in the schools so children understand the dangers of using GAI technology to create nude or sexually explicit images of their classmates.

In conclusion, I would like to thank you again for this opportunity to appear before the Subcommittee to discuss the dangers around GAI technology in its current unregulated state and what that presents to children online. NCMEC is eager to continue working with this Subcommittee and other Members of Congress to find solutions to these issues that I have shared with you today, and I look forward to your questions.

Ms. MACE. Thank you. I will now recognize Mr. Szabo to please begin your opening statement.

Statement of Carl Szabo
Vice President and General Counsel Netchoice

Mr. SZABO. Thank you. Madam Chair, Ranking Member Connolly, my name is Carl Szabo. I am Vice President and General Counsel of Netchoice. I am also an adjunct professor at George Mason Antonin Scalia Law School.

The stories that I have heard so far are horrible and terrifying, and it enrages me as a father of two that a principal is more willing to side with the perpetrators of a bad action than the victim. I think that is little outside what I am here to talk about, but fundamentally, we should support principals who enforce rules, not principals who try to escape responsibility.

Just kind of jumping in, I do want to kind of disagree a little with my colleague over here. AI is heavily regulated today. It is heavily regulated today. Every law that applies offline applies online. So, when it comes to harassment, we need to enforce harassment law. When it comes to fraud, we need to enforce fraud law. Good example is Sam Bankman-Fried went to prison not because of crypto, but because of fraud. So, the notion that AI is some escape clause for criminals, I think, is incorrect, and we need to do more law enforcement and more prosecution of bad actors.

Simple example, and I kind of outline this in my testimony, so, there was a famous situation this past couple of months where President Biden up in New Hampshire allegedly sent out a bunch of robocalls saying he was dropping out of the race. They used AI to generate the robocalls. Well, turns out that Pindrop, a company that detects AI-generated content, detected it, identified it was created by ElevenLabs, contacted them. Law enforcement then got the name of the perpetrator from ElevenLabs and arrested him. And they arrested him, not under any new law, but New Hampshire law, for example, makes it a crime to engage in such fraud. The Telecommunications Privacy Act, TCPA, makes it illegal. We have Federal laws with prison sentences up to 20 years for such criminal activity. So, I do not care if you use a robot, or you do it yourself, or you get an impersonator from ''Saturday Night Live,'' fraud is fraud, and we need to be willing to prosecute it.

But that is not saying that there are not gaps in the law. I think you are correct. When it comes to things like child sexual abuse material, there are existing gaps in law, and we have been working at Netchoice with lawmakers across the country to close those gaps. Under existing CSAM law, you actually require an actual photo, a real photograph of child sexual abuse material, to be prosecuted. So, bad actors are taking photographs of minors, using AI to modify them into sexually compromised positions, and then escaping the letter of the law. Not the purpose of the law, but the letter of the law. So, this is an example where legislation that is before Congress, that Chairwoman Mace has introduced and many others, can help fill those gaps and make sure that bad actors go to prison.

Looking to the issue of nonconsensual deepfakes, this is something we are also working with state lawmakers across the country to make sure that we enact laws. And one of the things that we did at Netchoice, we sat down, and we looked at First Amendment law because the last thing we want to do is create a law that does not hold up in court. We do not want a criminal to get prosecuted and then have a get-out-of-jail free card because we did not artfully address some of the constitutional challenges. So, when we sat down and drafted, and it is included in the back end of our testimony, some of our proposed recommendations, we identified the constitutional issues and then filled in those gaps.

Finally, when it comes to artificial intelligence, deepfakes, anything like that, we need to make sure we get the definitions correct. One of the challenges that we are seeing across the country, many states have introduced legislation, well intentioned, but, unfortunately, their definition of ‘‘artificial intelligence’’ is written so broadly, it would apply to a calculator or a refrigerator. And so, we need to make sure when we are drafting definitions and we are writing legislation, that we need to hit the target directly. Otherwise, we risk creating a law that is unconstitutional, and an unconstitutional law will protect no Americans.

Just to close out. The last thing that I will chime in on, and I am happy to answer your questions about what is going on at the state level, challenges we can address, but legislation must come from the legislative branch of government. One of the things that truly scares me is when we see executive overreach try to seize control of certain sectors of the government, and the fundamental problem is, like what we have seen in the latest executive order on AI, as well intentioned as it may or may not be, it will violate the major questions doctrine.

So, once again, unconstitutional laws will protect no one. Laws must be written by the legislature and enforced by the executive branch. And to that end, I fully welcome the opportunity to work with this legislature on creating laws that protect everyone from AI deepfakes.

Ms. MACE. Thank you. I will now recognize Dr. Waldman to begin your opening statement.

Statement of Dr. Ari Ezra Waldman Professor of Law University of California’s Irvine School of Law

Dr. WALDMAN. Thank you. Chairwoman Mace, Ranking Member Connolly, and Members of the Subcommittee, thank you for the opportunity to provide testimony about the dangers of and possible responses to deepfakes here today. My name is Ari Waldman, and I am a professor of law at the University of California at Irvine, where I research, among other things, the impact of new technologies on marginalized populations. Given my commitment to these issues and my own personal experience with image-based abuse, I also sit on the board of directors of the Cyber Civil Rights Initiative, or CCRI, the leading nonprofit organization dedicated to combating image-based sexual abuse and other technology-facilitated harms. Although I sit on the board of CCRI, I am here in my own capacity as an academic and as a researcher.

As we have already heard, AI means, in this context, we have a proliferation problem in which images that are fake images and synthetic images and videos about anyone, whether it is Taylor Swift or a young teenage girl, can be sent throughout the internet within moments. Technology, of course, did not create this problem, but it certainly made the problem bigger, harder to identify and dismiss, and vastly more common. But common does not mean that harm is evenly distributed.

Deepfakes cause unique harms that are disproportionately experienced by women, particularly those who are intersectionally marginalized, like Black women and trans women. So much of the history of modern technology begins with men wanting to objectify and sexualize women. It is no wonder that recent advances in deep-learning technology is reflecting our cultural and institutional biases against women. Even here, the story Mrs. Mani tells us about how a school is inappropriately ending up putting the female victim at risk reminds me of how so many schools approach the harassment of women, of trans women, of Black women and queer folk, generally.

The people who create, solicit, and distribute deepfake porn of women and girls have many motives, but what they all have in common is a refusal to see their victims as full and equal persons. Like other forms of sexual exploitation, deepfake porn is used to punish, silence, and humiliate mostly women, pushing them out of the public sphere and away from positions of power and influence. Let us be clear: this is not mere speech. This is not protected by the First Amendment. The harm caused by artificial, nonconsensual pornography is virtually indistinguishable from the harm caused by actual nonconsensual pornography: extreme psychological distress that can lead to self-harm and suicide; physical endangerment that include in-person stalking and harassment; and financial, professional, and reputational ruin.

There are new deepfake porn apps and web services that launch every month, and platforms do not seem willing to do anything about them. These services produce thousands of images every week, and those images are shared on websites that Google and other platforms list in their results and prominently do so. And as we know, deepfakes go viral, even for someone as famous as Taylor Swift. It is always the last bastion of those who want a deregulatory agenda to say that we need to enforce current laws and we do not need any new laws, but we already know and have examples, and many examples, of current laws not even working. Simply enforcing the laws that we have is insufficient.

Although most of us around the world relate to Taylor Swift's music, almost none of us have the same resources at our disposal as she does. If digital forgeries of us get out there, we are often powerless. That is not just because we cannot all afford lawyers, nor is it just because we do not have lawmakers or platforms listening to us. It is because, just like with real nonconsensual pornography, it is extremely difficult to mitigate the harm of deepfakes after the fact. This means we need deterrence. We need to stop this, particularly nonconsensual deepfake pornography, before it starts, and that is where Congress can step in.

The First Amendment does not stand in the way of Congress acting. There is longstanding precedent in First Amendment law for regulating false harmful expression that is perceived by others to be true. While false expression that is clearly not harmful or likely to be mistaken for real depictions of individuals, such as parody or satire, enjoy considerable First Amendment protection, there is nothing about defamation and fraud that has been historically considered protected by the First Amendment. So, I am not sure what the deep, difficult conversation is here about trying to pass a law that passes First Amendment scrutiny because nothing that we are talking about here is protected by the First Amendment. There are criminal prohibitions against impersonation, against counterfeiting and forgery, and these have never raised serious constitutional concerns.

I would argue that the intentional distribution of sexually explicit, photorealistic visual material that appears to depict an actual, identifiable individual without that individual's consent should be prohibited. Civil penalties are a step forward toward deterrence but insufficient. Deepfakes offer a liar's dividend, as the legal scholars Danielle Citron and Bobby Chesney have argued. In a world where we cannot tell the difference between true and false, those that are lying have a leg up. Thank you.

Ms. MACE. Thank you all. I will now recognize myself for 5 minutes for questioning. And to piggyback on Dr. Waldman, yes, that Taylor Swift video got 45 million views before it was ever taken down, and there are people today who do not know that it was a deepfake, probably believe that it was still real because they do not know the difference and did not know it was taken down because it was a deepfake. So, I appreciate everyone's points today.

My first questions will go to Mrs. Mani, and first of all, I just want to say as a mom of a 14-year-old girl, it is horrifying to know what your daughter went through and the fact that they released the names. I did not have that detail, but it really pains me to hear that. I was raped at the age of 16 by a classmate of mine in high school. I dropped out of school shortly thereafter, and I can only imagine as a mom what my mom felt at the time. It is a deeply painful experience, and I am really sorry that it happened to you and any woman or young girl that has gone through this. I hate, you know, what they have felt and the shame that they have gone through. And on that point, when George Stephanopoulos rape shamed me on Sunday on ''ABC News This Week,'' I want to make sure that no woman or girl is ever treated that way, and I hope that we can put a stop to that.

So, first of all, my first question to you, in your written testimony about what was done to your daughter, you state this event left her feeling helpless and powerless. As a mom, can you talk to us a little bit about what this has done to your family?

Ms. MANI. Yes. So, I probably will not share what you want to hear, but the moment when Francesca was informed——

Ms. MANI. Mm-hmm.

Ms. MANI [continuing]. By her counselor and her vice principal that she was one of the AI victims, she did feel helpless and powerless.

Ms. MACE. Mm-hmm.

Ms. MANI. And then she went out from the office, and she has noticed group of boys making fun of group of girls that were very emotional in the hallway. In that second, she turned from sad to mad, and now, because of you, all of you, we feel very empowered because I think you guys are listening. And just like you pointed out, you are a father. I think we are all human beings, we all have children, and we all have brothers and sisters that we want to protect, and we should sit down together and figure out a way how to fix it.

And I am so sorry that Mr. Stephanopoulos shamed you. I think that is the narrative that must change in media. Besides upsetting, it is just irresponsible and dangerous. The narrative needs to be changed.

Ms. MACE. Mm-hmm.

Ms. MANI. And instead of talking about girls and how they feel as a victim, we should be talking about the boys and how are they being empowered by the people in power, especially, in my case, in education, by being left unaccountable, walking the hallways with the girls. My daughter does not mind. I do.

Ms. MACE. Right, and I want to thank you for your and your daughter's advocacy, too. Your voice is very important because this is so early on in terms of the technology and what laws we are looking at, at the Federal and the state level. It is very important to hear voices of moms and dads and parents and the kids who have been affected, quite frankly, because those voices have to be a part of the conversation, and I hope that your advocacy will help change the policies not just at her school, but at every school. So, we really admire and appreciate you being here today.

I have less than 2 minutes, and I did want to, while I have you, Mr. Szabo, talk about legislatively, policy wise, because I am very, very, very, very tuned in to, one, as a victim of sexual trauma and assault and then seeing, you know, the things that I have seen, especially over the last couple of months, the advent of technology and then nonconsensual pornographic images and videos, et cetera, and then digital forgeries. You know, at the Federal and the state level, just at the state level, how many states have updated their laws so far?

Mr. SZABO. So, right now, we have been working with states across the country. Wisconsin is about to enact the two recommended pieces.

Ms. MANI. Are they the first?

Mr. SZABO. I do not want to say they are the first——

Ms. MACE. Mm-hmm.

Mr. SZABO [continuing]. But they are definitely one of the leaders on this. They are going to actually enact both the recommended Stop Deepfake CSAM Act as well as the Stop Nonconsensual Artificially Generated Images Act. California right now, we are working with lawmakers out there to make sure that their introduced legislation does not get thrown out by a court when a bad actor gets arrested. And so, we are seeing many states across the country start to adopt this. To your home state of South Carolina, I would love to see—

Ms. MACE. That is what I was going to bring up—I have 40 seconds left—is talking about South Carolina's laws, and I am going to look up impersonations and forgeries. I am not quite as familiar with state law. Obviously, that is not my jurisdiction. But when I looked at what was going on, when I found out about these women in my district that had been recorded without their knowledge or consent, I looked at state law. State Law 16–17–470 is under peeping Tom voyeurism laws. A $500 fine and up to 3 years in jail for the first offense is offensive. It is not a felony until the second offense, but clearly it is not enough, but there is not digital. There is nothing that would include, I believe, deepfakes in there, so I would love to talk to you about and actually even work with our state legislature, who I know our state legislature is working on revenge porn laws, but I also want to strengthen state law in all ways with nonconsensual images and video. So, I would love to talk to you afterwards, so thank you. I am going to yield back to my colleague from Virginia, Mr. Connolly.

Mr. CONNOLLY. Thank you. Mr. Shehan, I just want you to know, you could not pay me a million dollars a month to have your job. I cannot imagine dealing every day with violence against, abuse against children. It is just horrifying and very hard to listen to or contemplate, and I salute you for doing what you are doing and protecting children.

Dr. Waldman, well, it is almost St. Patrick's Day, a little leprechaun on my shoulder. You will forgive this question, but is deepfakes mentioned in the Constitution of the United States?

Dr. WALDMAN. No.

Mr. CONNOLLY. No. So, according to Samuel Alito logic, we have no ability to regulate deepfakes because it is not mentioned in the Constitution. Isn't that kind of what he did in the Dobbs decision with respect to abortion?

Dr. WALDMAN. Yes. There is no history and tradition of regulating deepfake technology under his theory of interpretation.

Mr. CONNOLLY. Thank you. So much for originalism. Of course, we saw a lot of originalism with respect to the Fourteenth Amendment just recently. I think it is kind of outside the window, Antonin Scalia Law School being named after an originalist notwithstanding. Mr. Szabo, if I understood him correctly, was suggesting we do not really need a lot of new laws. There are some gaps, but how about enforcing what we got both at the state level and the Federal level. What is your sense of that? I am addressing you, Dr. Waldman.

Dr. WALDMAN. Oh, sorry.

Mr. CONNOLLY. I mean, Congress is all about passing laws. Do we need to pass more laws? I mean, are there, in fact, some significant gaps that allow malign things to happen that we could perhaps prevent.

Dr. WALDMAN. Especially in this situation. We have seen it before with nonconsensual pornography. We needed new laws on the books because existing defamation or existing tort law had too many gaps, especially when victims originally allowed the image to be taken or video to be taken in the context of a consensual relationship but then distributed without their consent. So, we needed new laws, and we have seen some progress. My colleague at GW Law School, Mary Anne Franks, has been a leader in working with legislatures to pass legislation all across the country, so that is just one example. There are so many gaps here as well.

Mr. CONNOLLY. So, I invite you to provide us a list of those gaps because we would be glad to work on filling those legislative gaps.

I know my colleague and friend, Mr. Raskin, has to go to another committee. I yield the balance of my time to Mr. Raskin.

Mr. RASKIN. Well, thank you very much, Mr. Connolly. I just had one question for Mr. Waldman. Can you tell us what is the experience of deepfake regulatory legislation in the states and have they survived First Amendment attack, and what is the best model for creating a statute to deal with the problem?

Dr. WALDMAN. So, we do not have a lot of examples of state legislation focusing specifically on deepfakes, but we have examples of state legislation focusing on nonconsensual pornography that has gone to be challenged on First Amendment grounds, and they have been upheld. Minnesota is a really good example. The State Supreme Court handed down—and Illinois—handed down excellent decisions saying that, just as I discussed in my written testimony, there is no reason why this kind of nonconsensual harmful activity has ever been protected by the First Amendment. And Congressman Connolly, you are talking about history and tradition. Here, we have an example. There is no history and tradition of allowing this type of content, this type of behavior to be protected by the First Amendment.

Mr. RASKIN. Thank you very much. I yield back, and thank you, Mr. Connolly.

Mr. CONNOLLY. Thank you, Mr. Raskin. Mr. Szabo, you know, I represent George Mason University, though I would never have named law schools the way it got named. It is a public university. But I invite you to do the same thing I have invited Dr. Waldman to do, which is, where there are gaps, or, for that matter, where there are enforcement issues, please alert us. You may want to comment.

Mr. SZABO. Yes, thank you. So, first of all, with respect to the gaps, I highly suggest we take a look at making sure that our laws clearly address AI deepfake CSAM, one such example. The other, when it comes to law enforcement. So, this is something that— there is a group called Stop Child Predators that put out a report recently. Ninety-nine percent of reports of child sexual abuse material do not even get investigated. Yes, I know. Only one percent of reports of child sexual abuse material get investigated, and that is a lack of resource. So, there is currently legislation, both on the House and Senate side from both parties, called the Invest in Child Safety Act, which would give law enforcement more tools to put bad actors behind bars, and that is something I suggest taking a look at as well.

Mr. CONNOLLY. And I would just say in closing, when I was Chairman of Fairfax County, we had a police unit that looked at, you know, child predation and sex trafficking and crimes against children, but that was 15 years ago, and what has happened with technology has just exploded. And often, I think it just goes beyond the resources of local law enforcement to monitor, let alone entirely enforce, so I think that is something we are going to look at in terms of how can we find better ways of addressing the issue at that level. Thank you so much.

Ms. MACE. Thank you. I will now recognize Mr. Timmons for 5 minutes.

Mr. TIMMONS. Thank you, Madam Chair. Mr. Szabo, you said that we do not really need a lot of new laws, and, Dr. Waldman, you have taken a pretty different stance on that. I mean, it seems to me that there are, indeed, holes and there are gaps, whether it is revenge porn, nonconsensual porn, child porn. I mean, I think, Mr. Szabo, you would agree that we do need to address that. I mean, there is just a lot of gray area surrounding causes of action and ways to be made whole, whether it is using civil law to extract financial benefits or criminal law in certain circumstances. But you would agree that we do need to address the holes as it relates to those areas.

Mr. SZABO. Hundred percent. I mean, you have laws like FCRA, HIPAA, all these laws. Rohit Chopper is the director of the CFPB. He and I probably disagree on not much. Even he recognizes that you cannot hide behind a computer because existing laws apply, but here we do have gaps that do need to be filled.

Mr. TIMMONS. So, I guess to that, I mean, are you familiar with the Coalition for Content Provenance and Authenticity that Adobe has founded?

Mr. SZABO. Yes.

Mr. TIMMONS. OK. So, I mean, it seems that one of the big problems is that anybody can use the internet and create deepfakes of any kind, and there is no way of knowing who created it, and that is a big challenge.

Mr. SZABO. Exactly. So, what we need to do is better identify the perpetrators. I completely agree that it is a challenge, but you can reverse engineer. You can look at IP addresses. That is kind of what happened with the Biden deepfake call. Once they——

Mr. TIMMONS. I wanted to go to that.

Mr. SZABO. Yes.

Mr. TIMMONS. So, they were able to charge them because it was fraudulent in that he was not actually pulling out of the race, and there are all kind of laws associated with that. Would it be illegal if the same individual, instead of saying that the President was pulling out of the race, did dozens of videos of him falling upstairs or stammering or stuttering? I mean, you know, those will have equally adverse impacts on a campaign. What law would apply if somebody did a video of him falling into Marine One or falling out of Marine one?

Mr. SZABO. Yes.

Mr. TIMMONS. I mean, is that illegal?

Mr. SZABO. It is a complex——

Mr. TIMMONS. The answer is no.

Mr. SZABO. Yes.

Mr. TIMMONS. I do not think it is.

Mr. SZABO. Well, ''it depends,'' is kind of the problem because you have the public figure doctrine. You have satire. There is a lot that goes into that. States have tried to look at this by requiring campaign videos that use altered images to have a disclosure, but the challenge there, again, is in the definition. So, if a politician were standing in front of a green screen, that would be defined as an altered image, and all of a sudden you have to put at the bottom of your campaign ad, there are fake images in the campaign ad.

Mr. TIMMONS. Again, I mean, there are so many different bizarre media outlets. I mean, you could not put a video of a fake video of the President falling, which, again, there are many that exist that are not fake. But I mean, if you had a fake one, you could not put it on television because it gets vetted through legal. You could not theoretically run an ad on a radio that is fabricated because the radio station has liability if they are going to release an ad that is fake, I mean. But, again, the internet is such a wide area of media consumption, that none of these laws really have any enforcement mechanism. I mean, how would you address a deepfake that would be detrimental to someone's political campaign or life, short of nonconsensual pornography, but still is equally bad? We do not have laws for that.

Mr. SZABO. Well, so you could bring an action under existing tort law for defamation of character, misappropriation.

Mr. TIMMONS. Why is it defamation if you are falling over?

Mr. SZABO. Because if it is not a real image, it is a——

Mr. TIMMONS. What if I fell over in a different image?

Mr. SZABO. Well, so, I was going to say——

Mr. TIMMONS. Again, truth is the ultimate defense to defamation, so.

Mr. SZABO. Yes. So, when it comes to nonconsensual disclosures, for example, you have the Hulk Hogan v. Gawker example that played out under existing privacy law, so there is potential there. There are a lot of laws out there that can be enforced today, and to the extent that we do find gaps, we need to make sure that when we fill them, that we do so in a constitutional way.

Mr. TIMMONS. I agree with you on that, and I think one thing that we are not talking about is disparity of resources. Dr. Waldman, you touched on this. Taylor Swift has unlimited resources. She can sue whoever she wants. If a similar situation to Ms. Mani happened, technically, under the VAWA civil cause of action, you could probably allege that it was nonconsensual pornography, I mean, but it would cost tens of thousands of dollars, so, I mean, I like loser pays across the board. But could we look into some sort of loser pays funding mechanism to address civil causes of action for revenge porn, nonconsensual porn, all of these things. Dr. Waldman, is that something——

Dr. WALDMAN. Yes, absolutely. I believe Chairwoman Mace's proposal includes a fee-shifting provision for civil damages that would, you know, it is found to be indeed nonconsensual, deepfake pornography, that the perpetrator would have to pay. But still, even Taylor Swift still has the problem of those images and videos are still out there, and even she cannot—

Mr. TIMMONS. Well, it also goes back to the provenance. Like, how do you know who did it? Anyways, OK. I am over. Thank you. I yield back.

Ms. MACE. Thank you, and I will recognize Ms. Pressley for 5 minutes.

Ms. PRESSLEY. Thank you to our witnesses for being here today, including Ms. Mani. As a survivor of intra-family childhood sexual abuse myself, I must say, I really do look forward to a day where families and children do not have to weaponize and relive their trauma in order to compel action from their government, but I am grateful for those who do it time and time again.

Frederick Douglass once said it is easier to build strong children than to repair broken men and women. That is why in the 116th Congress, as a freshman Member and serving on the Oversight Committee, I convened the first-ever hearing on childhood trauma in the history of this Committee. Children across the country and in my district, the Massachusetts 7th, are facing layered crises, shouldering unprecedented emotional burden from challenges in their homes, classrooms, and now, more than ever, online. Our young girls—our young girls, and we must see them as all of our children—our girls are targeted and victimized the most.

Just last year, the CDC released a report that teenage girls are experiencing record-high levels of violence, sadness, and suicide ideation. The trauma backpacks that they carry across the thresholds into our schools every day only grow heavier. I ask unanimous consent to enter this youth risk behavior survey into the record.

Ms. MACE. Without objection.

Ms. PRESSLEY. You know, as a Black woman who was once a Black young girl, I know intimately what it is for your body to be criminalized, your hair to be criminalized, for your body to be banned, objectified, and, as a survivor, violated. And as this report makes plain and this hearing has confirmed, our girls are being traumatized. I worry for my 15-year-old daughter, who will think that it is normal, a conflated part of her identity as a girl or a woman in this country, to experience these indignities and these violations. Professor Waldman, in what ways does nonconsensual, deepfake pornography contribute to the growing crises of childhood trauma?

Dr. WALDMAN. I need more than 2 1/2 minutes to describe all those ways, but very briefly, the nonconsensual, deepfake pornography does more than just nonconsensual pornography in that not only does it objectify and make someone at risk of, you know, someone who is always looking over their shoulder, every image, every social encounter that they engage in, which deters them from engaging with other people, which is necessary at any age of life, but also, it allows for this to happen even if you do not have any images out there, right, because these images can be created even with a simple instruction to an AI generator. Essentially, what it does is it creates perpetual trauma and perpetual risk of trauma.

Ms. PRESSLEY. That is right. Thank you. And further, a traumatized child certainly has a decreased readiness to learn. Advances in AI have made it easier for people to create sexual content that intimidates, degrades, dehumanizes, and traumatizes victims, and this technology is becoming more present in our K through 12 schools. Ms. Mani, can you describe what the psychological damage is for teenagers who are victims of this type of harassment? And once again, thank you for the courage you and your daughter continue to display in the face of these reprehensible acts.

Ms. MANI. [Off mic.]

Ms. MACE. Turn your microphone on or speak into it.

Ms. MANI. So, I am not trained to really talk about the repercussions of those images. All I can tell you is that we are not the majority. We took a stand and my daughter took back her dignity, but not many girls can be in the same position because of multiple of layers and factors. Most importantly, it is a shame that in 2024, we are still talking about consent, consent in regards to our body. Now that should be taught as a sentence, and our girls that are not empowered but rather falling through the cracks because of the educational system. Laws, they have to be put in place? Hundred percent. School policies? Hundred percent. And then we all should sit down and figure out ways of how to make it better without pointing fingers as well but, rather, because it is ethical and the right thing to do.

Ms. PRESSLEY. Absolutely. I think we should start with trauma-informed schools. Thank you.

Ms. MANI. Hundred percent.

Ms. MACE. I will now recognize Mr. Langworthy for 5 minutes. Mr. LANGWORTHY. Thank you, Chairwoman Mace. It seems now every single week that goes by, we see another story about a bad actor using AI unethically. And while I strongly support innovation and will always work to make sure that this country does not lose its edge to China in the AI race, I think that we all must hold accountable unethical creators, criminal actors, and especially those who are creating child pornography and child sexual abuse material.

Emerging technology should always be used in ethical ways, and tech companies, alongside Congress, need to ensure that this happens. That is why I am very proud to be working on legislation with attorney generals [sic] from all 50 states and four territories that would create a commission examining generative AI safeguards, assess current statutes, and recommend legislative revisions to enhance law enforcement's ability to prosecute AI-related child exploitation crimes.

And I would like to enter into the record a letter signed by 54 attorneys general calling for this commission-based approach.

Ms. MACE. Without objection.

Mr. LANGWORTHY. I want to start today by talking about law enforcement's approach to generative AI. Mr. Shehan, how is law enforcement reacting to the uptick in AI-generated child sexual abuse material, CSAM? Has that approach been reactive as in waiting for images to circulate, or are there ways law enforcement can be more proactive?

Mr. SHEHAN. Excellent question. In a lot of the scenarios, these are reactive because I outlined earlier that many of the generative AI technology companies, they are not taking proactive measures to identify and stop the creation of that material on the onset. It is often after the content has already made its way into the wild that you have social media companies and the such that are finding these types of material and reporting it into our CyberTipline, and we, in turn, provide that information to the Internet Crimes Against Children Task Force members who are actively investigating these cases.

One quick example, in the fourth quarter of last year, we had a report that came through—it was made by Facebook—regarding an adult male who was talking through Messenger to a minor using Stable Diffusion to create child sexual abuse content. Sent it to the minor. It was detected and reported. The

Wisconsin ICAC investigated that case, found out not only was he creating content, possessed child sexual abuse material, and through the forensic interviews, also realized he was abusing his 5-year-old son. State and local law enforcement are having to deal with these issues because the technology companies are not taking the steps on the front end to build these tools with Safety By Design. We are getting this content out into the wild far too early, and something has to be done about this.

Mr. LANGWORTHY. It is chilling. Thank you. I would like to point out that the sheer volume of cyber tips has oftentimes prevented law enforcement from pursuing proactive investigation efforts that would efficiently target the most egregious offenders. In only a 3- month period from November 1, 2022 to February 1, 2023, there were over 99,000 IP addresses throughout the United States that distributed known CSAM, and only 782 were investigated. Currently, law enforcement, through no fault of their own, they just do not have the ability to investigate and prosecute the overwhelming number of these cases.

Mr. Szabo, there have been several bills introduced this Congress to address the current legal framework to protect those exploited by generative AI, and even more that look to combat deepfakes all at once. You know, while many of them are well intentioned, my concern is that the Department of Justice has not had much success in prosecuting a number of these cases because of the fine line that needs to be walked with the First Amendment rights. So, I wanted to ask you, what are the biggest gaps in the current legal framework that need to be filled?

Mr. SZABO. So, there is a case called Ashcroft v. Freedom of Speech Coalition, and basically what it got into is an overly broad law, well intentioned, to prohibit these types of activities, but it applied to non-actual victims of fake images, and the U.S. Supreme Court shot that down. They said it is a violation of the First Amendment. So, one of the gaps is the type of legislation that we have been talking about here, whether it is the Chairwoman's legislation as well as some of the other bills that have been proposed from all sides of the aisle, to kind of fill that gap and make crystal clear that AI-created content, if it has the image of an actual or identifiable child, is CSAM material, as opposed to the way the laws are currently written, which requires an actual photo. So, we are seeing time and time again that bad actors are escaping justice. At the same time, the Invest in Child Safety Act, I think, is a really important one to give law enforcement the tools it needs.

One other thing to address is groups like NCMEC are taking on tons of information but not necessarily having enough time to process it, and they have a mandatory deletion time for content. So, giving them a bit more time to process and prosecute content that they receive and tips that they receive, I think would be helpful as well.

Mr. LANGWORTHY. Thank you very much, and I am out of time. Thank you, Chairwoman, for having this hearing, and I yield back.

Ms. MACE. Thank you. I will now recognize Mr. Garcia for 5 minutes.

Mr. GARCIA. Thank you very much, Madam Chair, and thank you for allowing me to waive on to the Committee today. I want to thank all of our witnesses, particularly to Ms. Mani. My heart goes out to you and everything that obviously you have experienced. I also want to just note a couple other cases I think are important. A few weeks ago, fake images were circling online that put real students' faces on artificially generated nude bodies from Beverly Vista Middle School in Beverly Hills. We are talking about middle school students. We know that that is completely predatory and unacceptable. I know a lot of examples have been discussed today. Also, just weeks ago, AI-generated pornographic deepfake images of Taylor Swift were viewed more than 45 million times.

Now, media investigations showed how easy it was to get AI software guardrails to post these images and how platforms struggled to prevent people from sharing them.

Ms. MACE. Will the gentleman yield for 1 second? We need to waive you on. I ask unanimous consent to have Representative Garcia from California on the Subcommittee for today's hearing, and without objection so ordered.

Mr. GARCIA. Thank you. Now, I would like to ask unanimous consent to introduce this article entitled, ''The Taylor Swift Deepfake Debacle Was Preventable,'' and these are all really serious issues. Now, fortunately, someone like Taylor Swift had millions of fans that came out to defend her, to protect her online. They flooded social media with junk posts to bury abusive content. The phrase, ''Protect Taylor Swift,'' was on 36,000 posts that were shared. But we know that Taylor Swift fans and Swifties cannot protect everyone and certainly not people that do not have that platform, and so Congress has a responsibility to act.

Now, deepfake pornography accounts for 98 percent of deepfake videos online, and 99 percent of all deepfake porn features women, while only 1 percent feature men. A 2019 study found that 96 percent of all deepfake videos were nonconsensual pornography, and it does not matter, of course, whether you are a billionaire, one of the most powerful women on earth, whether you are Taylor Swift, or a middle school student, deepfake pornography and the manipulation of images is deeply troubling and predatory, particularly to women across this country and girls.

Now, we know that deepfake images can also be used to intimidate, harass, and victimize people, and oftentimes, if you are targeted, there is nowhere to turn, and, Ms. Mani, I know in your situation you received little to no support. And I just wanted to ask you, did you feel you got any support from the actual school itself?

Ms. MANI. I received zero support, and it is disappointing that I have to sit down in here, and, you know, fighting for the girls of Westfield and other girls of United States because my school did not have the balls to do so. Also, in contrast, as you mentioned, the Beverly Hills incident, that principal or superintendent, you know, withdrew the boys from the school, completed HIB investigation within 10 days. He did the right thing. Was it an easy choice? No, but it was the right thing, and I think our girls should not be solo gladiators fighting for their rights. It is shameful that in 2024, we need to fight still for our rights.

Mr. GARCIA. That is exactly right, and I want to note that the Beverly Hills middle school case, I mean, students were actually expelled in that that case.

Ms. MANI. Correct.

Mr. GARCIA. The principal acted quickly.

Ms. MANI. That is right.

Mr. GARCIA. And it is important to note, I mean, all young girls deserve equal protection. That also happens to be a school that is very well resourced with parents that are constantly advocating. It is in Beverly Hills, and so it should not matter where the school is or the resources parents may have, but every girl deserves protection at every single school or any student, period.

Also, just, Professor Waldman, we know, also, just briefly, with the remainder of my time, we know that Russia and China and other hostile actors are targeting our elections. We have seen deepfakes already used to do that, whether it is targeting President Biden or other elections that are happening as well. Can you explain how what is happening right now is undermining our election security and as well as our national security?

Dr. WALDMAN. Sure. So, I think it can boil down to what deepfakes do is, as I said during my testimony, they create a liar's dividend, which means that when anything could be false, then everything is presumed to be false. Therefore, when we know that AI can be used by Russia and hostile countries to undermine our democracy, then we start disbelieving everything, right? We do not start just disbelieving the things that are actually false. We start then allowing people to say, well, how do I know that it is true? It could be a deepfake. And when we disagree on even just the basic things, democracy ceases to work.

Mr. GARCIA. And I appreciate that. I think obviously, deepfakes are oftentimes being used for entertainment purposes. I mean, look, I have seen deepfakes on funny videos, on things that could be entertaining, but it is also deeply troubling when it affects our elections and certainly when it is affecting people and young people in our country.

Before I close, I just want to introduce a written statement into the record from Dr. Mary Anne Franks. Dr. Franks is the President and Legislative Tech Policy Director of the Cyber Civil Rights Institute and Eugene L. and Barbara A. Bernard Professor of Intellectual Property, Technology, and Civil Rights at George Washington Law. So, I would like to just——

Ms. MACE. Without objection, so ordered.

Mr. GARCIA. Thank you, and thank you all to our witnesses.

Ms. MACE. Right. I will now recognize Mrs. Luna for 5 minutes.

Mrs. LUNA. Chairwoman, if I could submit this poster into the record.

Ms. MACE. Without objection, so ordered.

Mrs. LUNA. So, there has been a lot of talk today on CSAM, but for those who might be tuning in that might not know what that is, it is the creation of child sexual abuse materials from lifelike images of children. This situation has not only perpetuated the occurrence of child sexual exploitation in this country, but has also created a new legal question about how to effectively crack down on the practice to protect our children. And I bring this up because this was actually something that the FBI, in talking to them about cybercrimes, asked us to specifically look at because they are having issues currently prosecuting these really, really gross, sick individuals because, technically, a child is not hurt in the process because it is a generated image.

According to recent reports, thousands of AI-generated child sex images have been found on forums across the dark web. Some of these forums have even been found to have instructions that detail how other pedophiles can create their own AI-generated sex images, and I just want to point to the poster behind me.

[Chart]

Mrs. LUNA. If you see ''after COVID in 2020,'' and then you see this spike, this also, in my opinion, correlates with the rise and the, I think, evolution of AI getting better and better and better at generating these graphics and images, and you can see it is clearly not good for our kids. This has increased the speed and scale at which pedophiles create new CSAM. One report explained that in the creation of new images, pedophiles superimpose the face of children onto adult bodies using deepfakes and rapidly generate many images through one single command.

The importance of raising awareness of this problem speaks for itself. In one study of an online forum with over 3,000 members, over 80 percent of respondents stated that they would use or intended to use AI to create child sexual abuse images. This is concerning for child safety and makes law enforcement efforts to find victims and combat real world abuse much, much more important. My first question is for Mr. John Shehan. You previously stated in a report of CSAM, online platforms grew from 32 million in 2022 to 36 million in 2023. What factors do you think have contributed to this trend?

Mr. SHEHAN. That is an excellent question, and much of it is around just the global scale and ability to create and disseminate child sexual abuse material. This is truly a global issue. The 36 million reports last year, more than 90 percent were outside the United States, individuals using U.S. servers, but we are also seeing a massive increase in the number of reports that we are receiving regarding the enticement of children for sexual acts.

In your chart there, you know, in 2021, we had about 80,000 reports regarding the online enticement of children. Last year, it jumped up to 180,000 reports. Not even through the first quarter of this year, we are already over 100,000 reports regarding the enticement of children. Many of these cases are involving generative AI. Others are financial sextortion. So, there are individuals in countries like Nigeria and the Ivory Coast, and it is all about the money. They are blackmailing young boys to create a sexually explicit image, just that one image, and then they are after the money——

Mrs. LUNA. The deepfakes.

Mr. SHEHAN [continuing]. Significant amounts of money.

Mrs. LUNA. Just out of curiosity, because we have legislation. I know that I am cosponsoring Representative Mace's legislation in regard to deepfakes, but in regard to the No. 1 platform that you are finding that this is being circulated on, and I know that this has been a question of how do these online platforms moderate this content, what is the No. 1 platform that you are finding that is distributing this?

Mr. SHEHAN. Well, so GAI and deepfakes, it is a difficult question because some of the companies that are reporting the most are doing the most. I mentioned earlier OpenAI. They are setting the bar for what every single other generative AI company should be doing in this space. I also gave an example just a minute ago about Stable Diffusion, which is owned by Stability

AI. They are not even registered to report to the CyberTipline. So, we have a huge gap in some of these providers who are enabling individuals to create child sexual abuse content, and they are not even set up to report. So, it is difficult to give a top provider when there are so many that are not even doing a bare minimum.

Mrs. LUNA. So, what would you say the bare minimums are?

Mr. SHEHAN. Well, certainly taking proactive steps that, if someone is trying to use these tools to create child sexual abuse material or modify it or text prompts to create, they should not be allowing that to happen. We started off this session, Ranking Member Connolly had mentioned the Stanford Internet Observatory research that was done that discovered that there was child sexual abuse material in the training set of these data that was given to the OpenAI models to train on. How did that even happen?

Mrs. LUNA. Yes.

Mr. SHEHAN. How is their child sexual abuse material in the content that they are training on? So, there are so many things that we work backward on to rectify the situation that we are in right now.

Mrs. LUNA. OK. Well, I know parents might be tuning in, so I just ask you, and I am sure you would agree, but maybe not post pictures of your children on the web because right now, it is kind of the Wild West out there, and they could be exploited.

Mr. SHEHAN. There certainly are situations where even the benign photos, the clothed photos, as you heard earlier, are being used, run through these tools, and turned into nudity and pornographic content. So, it is a troubling time to be posting content online with some of these tools that are not built Safety By Design.

Mrs. LUNA. Thank you for your time. Chairwoman, I yield my time.

Ms. MACE. OK. We will now, finally, Mr. Morelle, recognize you, and thank you for being here this afternoon. Thank you for waiting so patiently.

Mr. MORELLE. Thank you, Madam Chair, and let me start by thanking you for holding this incredibly important hearing. And thank Ranking Member Connolly and both of you for allowing me to participate in this conversation, as well as thanking our witnesses for sharing their perspectives on this fast-growing and very, very dangerous issue, an issue that has been noted overwhelmingly, disproportionately affects women.

And I also want to acknowledge some familiar faces on the witness panel. I, first of all, want to thank Dorata Mani, a mother, powerful advocate and partner in the war to help prevent innocent people from being harmed by nonconsensual deepfake images. I have had the pleasure of meeting both Dorata and her 14-year-old daughter, Francesca, several times, including here in Washington, where they both courageously participated in a conversation with myself and Congressman Tom Kean on this topic.

I also want to thank the Cyber Civil Rights Initiative, represented here by Dr. Waldman, for their assistance in the drafting of my legislation, the Preventing Deepfakes of Intimate Images Act, which was originally introduced in 2022, long before anyone heard of what happened to Taylor Swift, and we reintroduced the bill in May 2023. On this Subcommittee alone, Members Connolly, Lynch, Langworthy, and Moskowitz are cosponsors.

And as I listen and learn from our witnesses panel this afternoon, the need has been clearly demonstrated for a comprehensive, and what I hope will be a bipartisan, solution to address the unique pain caused by the distribution of nonconsensual, intimate deepfake images, and as has been said, and I think bears repeating, made so much easier today by advances in both generative AI as well as hardware and the capability of even laptops to be able to do this. You know, years ago, you would need to have some sophistication. Nowadays, frankly, I think teenagers will be able to do it with very little training and very little time and energy.

I agree with much of what has been said by my colleagues. Over 50 Members have already supported my legislation, which will make sharing these images - it is comprehensive in the sense that it creates sharing of the images a criminal offense and also creates a private right of action for victims to seek relief. And I hope others, not only on the Subcommittee, but other Members will consider joining as well as we look to perhaps work on all these different proposals and blend them together.

Having said that, in just a couple of minutes, I want to start with a question for you, Mrs. Mani, and thank you, again, for sharing your story and for your thoughtful notes and commentary on a comprehensive solution. And throughout your testimony and other comments you have made publicly, you called attention to the work that needs to be done at the local and state level, within our education system particularly, and also focusing on artificial intelligence companies and what they need to do and their responsibilities. So, based on your experience discussing your story and what you have learned, how do you think Congress can help ensure that these entities are better prepared to combat the issue of nonconsensual deepfake pornography?

Ms. MANI. I actually think we should establish a roundtable without pointing fingers and ask them for solutions. They are the experts. They will teach us more than we can ever know. So, that is one. No. 2, create a coalition of companies, platforms that host the illegal content, like Google, Amazon, and few others, as well as the financial platforms that facilitate spread of that content, like Amex, Google, Visa, PayPal, et cetera, et cetera, to come to the table because it is the right thing to do.

You know, I have watched, just like every one of us watched, the Senate hearing, and every single platform said the same thing that you said today. We are fathers and we are mothers, and I think that is what we need to do. We need to sit down and figure out ways how to fix it without laws and legislations. Put laws and legislations in place, and then put accountability on the perpetrators or the bad actors.

Mr. MORELLE. Thank you. If I could ask you, Dr. Waldman, in the few seconds I have left, could you talk about the importance of a multipronged approach, civil and criminal, in whatever it is we ultimately decide to do here?

Dr. WALDMAN. Sure. I think a civil remedy approach is a step forward but insufficient for a couple of reasons. We cannot be sure that a simple threat of civil damages would be enough because so many of the perpetrators of this are, you know, the dude in the basement who is probably judgment proof, and so you will not be made whole by a civil remedy. Relying on a civil remedy alone puts the burden entirely on the victim, right, and civil litigation is really expensive, so when you are not Taylor Swift, as we said before, it is really hard to even start something like that. And then in certain situations, we have a history of under criminalizing bad things that happen to women, and intersectionally marginalized women, in particular.

So, while I think we need to be concerned about people in power misusing their power in certain situations, we want to make sure we criminalize this kind of behavior in other instances for important reasons, because it is so bad, because we need that deterrent effect. And I fear that without this comprehensive approach, including government organizations like CISA getting involved in helping platforms do what they should be doing on this, then we are going to leave victims without any recourse.

Mr. MORELLE. Thank you, Madam Chair, for your indulgence, and thanks for allowing me the opportunity to participate. I yield back.

Ms. MACE. Of course. Thank you. In closing, I want to thank our panelists once again for their testimony today, and I want to encourage you all, please stay in touch with this Committee, but with my office. I am deeply passionate about this issue. I come from a background in technology. When I got my first job, I was a programmer, and I have since been fighting for things, especially for women and kids, and this is a very important issue. I have seen this kind of thing have devastating consequences, even deadly consequences, when we are talking about nonconsensual pornography.

I want to piggyback on what Dr. Walden just talked about, civil damages not being enough. You are right. Any victim who is a victim of a nonconsensual image or video, real or deepfake, should know, should be able to take possession of that and know that it is never going to be seen anywhere ever again for the rest of their life, if that is what they want. But that is not really a thing today, I mean, because these things can be found online and everywhere. Once that is out, it is forever. And these victims should be allowed to get their content back, real or fake, if their image and their likeness is part of it, and know that it has been destroyed forever, from every device, any cloud, anywhere online.

And we are not there yet, and it is deeply troubling. So, civil damages are not enough, and in some cases, I mean, there is not even criminal action here. I mean, I look at the Violence Against Women Act, and it is just a civil right of action, not even criminal. I think if you are doing voyeurism at the Federal level, you got to be, like, over international water for it to be against Federal law under Title 18. Like, it is insane to me. And so, I am deeply passionate about trying to correct some of this, correct course, find the gaps, like, as you said, Mr. Szabo, on definitions. While we were sitting here today, I went into the South Carolina's Code of Laws, and I just looked up the word ''porn.'' It does not exist in South Carolina's Code of Law. So, when we are talking about definitions, I agree with you, there is room for improvement, there are gaps here, and I really want to figure out how we move forward in a bipartisan manner at the Federal level, but also with states.

Especially in my home state of South Carolina, there is a lot of work to do. Five hundred fine for voyeurism, the first time is a misdemeanor is wrong, and it is offensive, and it should be much more expensive. We want to make sure that a man who does that to over a dozen women in South Carolina does not ever do it again, and a $500 fine and 3 years in jail just does not cut it. And the law is not clear on whether or not, if it is the first offense or if, let us say, for example, an example that I shared, if it is over a dozen women, images and videos this individual took, if it would be a felony because it is multiple victims. The law is not clear. So, there certainly is, you know, definitely room for improvement in our state as well. And I looked up impersonations, forgery. Forgery in South Carolina law is only related to financial transactions, mostly.

So, there is just so much room to improve here, both at the Federal and the state level. I want you all to know that my office is very much keen on adding to our portfolio of legislation, constitutionally, as it makes sense, not overdoing it, but just the right amount so that victims are no longer victimized, or when they are, that it is quickly corrected.

So, with that and without objection, all Members will have 5 legislative days within which to submit materials and to submit additional written questions for the witnesses, which will be forwarded to the witnesses for their response.

Ms. MACE. So, if there is no further business, without objection, the Subcommittee stands adjourned, and thank you.

[Whereupon, at 3:53 p.m., the Subcommittee was adjourned.]

Chapter 3

To Protect National Security Against the Threats Posed by Deepfake Technology and to Provide Legal Recourse to Victims of Harmful Deepfakes*

Committee on the Judiciary, Committee on Energy and Commerce, and the Committee on Homeland Security

Ms. CLARKE of New York (for herself and Mr. IVEY) introduced the following bill; which was referred to the Committee on the Judiciary, and in addition to the Committees on Energy and Commerce, and Homeland Security, for a period to be subsequently determined by the Speaker, in each case for consideration of such provisions as fall within the jurisdiction of the committee concerned.

Be it enacted by the Senate and House of Representatives of the United States of America in Congress assembled,

SECTION 1. SHORT TITLE.

This Act may be cited as the "Defending Each and Every Person from False Appearances by Keeping Exploitation Subject to Accountability Act of 2023" or the "DEEPFAKES Accountability Act".

SEC. 2. TRANSPARENCY REQUIREMENTS.

(a) IN GENERAL. — Chapter 47 of title 18, United States Code, is amended by adding at the end the following:

---

* This is an edited, reformatted and augmented version of A BILL to protect national security against the threats posed by deepfake technology and to provide legal recourse to victims of harmful deepfakes, Publication No. H. R. 5586, dated September 20, 2023.

In: The Deepfake Dilemma
Editor: Ruben Faulkner
ISBN: 979-8-90134-122-3

"§ 1041. Advanced technological false personation record

"(a) IN GENERAL.—Except as provided in subsection (j), any person who, using any means or facility of interstate or foreign commerce, produces an advanced technological false personation record with the intent to distribute such record over the internet or knowledge that such record shall be so distributed, shall ensure such record, complies with—

"(1) the requirement under subsection (b); and

"(2)(A) in the case of an audiovisual record, the disclosure requirements under subsection (c);

"(B) in the case of a visual record, the disclosure requirements under subsection (d); or

"(C) in the case of an audio record, the disclosure requirements under subsection (e).

"(b) CONTENT PROVENANCE.—Any advanced technological false personation record which contains a moving visual element shall contain technologies, such as content provenance technologies, that clearly identify such record as containing altered audio or visual elements, or as having been entirely created through generative artificial intelligence or similar technologies.

"(c) AUDIOVISUAL DISCLOSURE.—Any advanced technological false personation records containing both an audio and a visual element shall include—

"(1) not less than 1 clearly articulated verbal statement that identifies the record as containing altered audio and visual elements, and a concise description of the extent of such alteration;

"(2) an unobscured written statement in clearly readable text appearing at the bottom of the image throughout the duration of the visual element that identifies the record as containing altered audio and visual elements, and a concise description of the extent of such alteration; and

"(3) a link, icon, or similar tool to signal that the content has been altered by, or is product of, generative artificial intelligence or similar technology.

"(d) VISUAL DISCLOSURE.—Any advanced technological false personation records exclusively containing a visual element shall include an unobscured written statement in clearly readable text appearing at the bottom of the image throughout the duration of the visual element that identifies the record as containing altered visual elements, and either—

"(1) a concise description of the extent of such alteration; or

"(2) a clearly visible link, icon, or similar tool to signal that the content has been altered by, or is the product of, generative artificial intelligence or similar technology.

"(e) AUDIO DISCLOSURE.—Any advanced technological false personation records exclusively containing an audio element shall include, at the beginning of such record, a clearly articulated verbal statement that identifies the record as containing altered audio elements and a concise description of the extent of such alteration, and in the event such record exceeds two minutes in length, not less than 1 additional clearly articulated verbal statement and additional concise description at some interval during each two-minute period thereafter.

"(f) PENALTY.—

"(1) CRIMINAL PENALTY.—

"(A) FAILURE TO DISCLOSE.—Whoever knowingly fails to comply with the requirements under subsection (a)—

"(i) with the intent to humiliate or otherwise harass the person falsely exhibited, provided the advanced technological false personation record contains sexual content of a visual nature and appears to feature such person engaging in such seual acts or in a state of nudity;

"(ii) with the intent to cause violence or physical harm, incite armed or diplomatic conflict, or interfere in an official proceeding, including an election, provided the advanced technological false personation record did in fact pose a credible threatof instigating or advancing such;

"(iii) in the course of criminal conduct related to fraud, including securities fraud and wire fraud, false personation, or identity theft; or

"(iv) by a foreign power, or an agent thereof, with the intent of influencing a domestic public policy debate, interfering in a Federal, State, local, or territorial election, or engaging in other acts which such power 23 may not lawfully undertake; shall be fined under this title, imprisoned for not more than 5 years, or both.

"(B) ALTERING DISCLOSURES.—Whoever knowingly alters an advanced technological false personation record to remove or meaningfully obscure the disclosures required under subsection (a) with the intent to distribute such altered record and—

"(i) with the intent to humiliate or otherwise harass the person falsely exhibited, provided the advanced technological false personation record contains sexual content of a visual nature and appears to feature such person engaging in such sexual acts or in a state of nudity;

"(ii) with the intent to cause violence or physical harm, incite armed or diplomatic conflict, or interfere in an official proceeding, including an election, provided the advanced technological false personation record did in fact pose a credible threatof instigating or advancing such;

"(iii) in the course of criminal conduct related to fraud, including securities fraud and wire fraud, false personation, or identity theft; or "(iv) by a foreign power, or an agent thereof, with the intent of influencing a domestic public policy debate, interfering in a Federal, State, local, or territorial election, or engaging in other acts which such power may not lawfully undertake; shall be fined under this title, imprisoned for not more than 5 years, or both.

"(2) CIVIL PENALTY.—

"(A) FAILURE TO DISCLOSE.—Any person who violates subsection (a) shall be subject to a civil penalty of up to $150,000 per record or alteration, as well as appropriate injunctive relief.

"(B) ALTERING DISCLOSURES.—Any person who alters an advanced technological false personation record to remove or meaningfully obscure the disclosures required under subsection (a) with the intent to distribute such altered record shall be subject to a civil penalty of up to $150,000 per record or alteration, as well as appropriate injunctive relief.

"(g) PRIVATE RIGHT OF ACTION.—

"(1) IN GENERAL.—Any person who has been exhibited as engaging in falsified material activity in an advanced technological false personation record may bring a civil action before the appropriate Federal district court for damages under paragraph (2) and injunctive relief under paragraph (3) against a person who violates subsection (a) or alters an advanced technological false personation record to remove or meaningfully obscure the disclosures required under subsection (a).

"(2) DAMAGES.—Damages shall consist of the greater of—

"(A) actual damages suffered by the living person or the affiliated corporation or entity, and any additional substantially derivative profits of the person who violated subsection (a) or altered an advanced technological false personation record to remove or meaningfully obscure the disclosures required under subsection (a);

"(B) $50,000 per record, if the living person or affiliated corporation or entity experienced a perceptible individual harm or faced a tangible risk of experiencing such harm;

"(C) $100,000 per record, if the living person or affiliated corporation or entity experienced a perceptible individual harm or faced a tangible risk of experiencing such harm and the record purported to depict extreme or outrageous conduct by the living person; or

"(D) $150,000 per record, if the advanced technological false personation record contains explicit sexual content of a visual nature intended to humiliate or otherwise harass the person falsely depicted as engaging in such sexual acts or in a state of nudity.

"(3) INJUNCTIVE RELIEF.—Injunctive relief under this subsection shall include a requirement to comply with subsection (a).

"(h) PRIVACY PROTECTIONS.—

"(1) FEDERAL ACTIONS.—In enforcing this section, the Attorney General shall, to the extent practicable, consult with living persons exhibited as engaging in falsified material activity in advanced technological false personation records regarding measures the Attorney General can reasonably undertake to protect the privacy of such persons and minimize additional public viewings of such records.

"(2) PRIVATE ACTIONS.—A court in which a private action is brought under subsection (g) shall permit the plaintiff, upon petition, to file the claim under seal if the plaintiff can demonstrate a reasonable likelihood that the creation of public records regarding the advanced technological false personation record would result in embarrassing or otherwise harmful publicization of the falsified material activity in an advanced technological false personation record.

"(i) RULES OF CONSTRUCTION.—

"(1) Nothing in this section shall be interpreted as authorizing the production of an advanced technological false personation record which includes disclosures if such record is otherwise prohibited by law or regulation.

"(2) The word 'advanced' within the term 'advanced technological false personation record' shall not be interpreted as narrowing the definition of such term.

"(3) Nothing in this section shall be interpreted as a defense against, or as preempting or limiting, any Federal, State, local, or territorial laws, regulations, or policies that prohibit, impose more stringent standards in relation to, or provide additional or alternative remedies or damages in relation to, the production or distribution of advanced technological false personation records, deepfakes, or related content, including criminal and civil laws relating to copyright, tortious conduct, and false personation.

"(j) EXCEPTIONS.—

"(1) DISCLOSURE.—The requirements under subsections (c), (d), and (e) shall not apply with respect to any advanced technological false personation record—

"(A) containing alternative disclosures regarding the falsity of the exhibited material activities which a reasonable person would deem to be more prominent than those required under subsection (c), (d), or (e), as the case may be;

"(B) during the process of producing such record, provided the ultimately distributed record is in compliance with such requirements;

"(C) which primarily contains images or sound recordings of actual persons, such as performing artists, and have not been substantially digitally modified;

"(D) created in connection with editing a motion picture, television, music, or similar production or creating a derivative production thereof, the original content of which was created prior to the enactment of this section, in which the person appearing provided consent to their original appearance;

"(E) appearing in a context such that a reasonable person would not mistake the falsified material activity for actual material activity of the exhibited living person, such as parody shows or publications, historical reenactments, or fictionalized radio, television, or motion picture programming; or

"(F) produced by an officer or employee of the United States, or under the authority thereof, in furtherance of public safety or national security.

"(2) DIGITAL CONTENT PROVENANCE.—The digital content provenance requirement under subsection (b) shall not apply with respect to any class of advanced technological false personation records which the Attorney General determines by regulation should be excluded from such requirement.

"(k) ADVISORY OPINIONS, WAIVER, AND STANDARDS.—

"(1) ADVISORY OPINIONS.—The Attorney General shall—

"(A) establish a process by which any producer of audio, visual, or audiovisual content may seek an advisory opinion from the Attorney General regarding whether their proposed production is required to comply with the requirements under this section;

"(B) respond to a request described in subparagraph (A) not later than 30 days after the date of submission; and

"(C) not pursue enforcement action under this section against any producer who relied in good faith on such an advisory opinion.

"(2) WAIVER.—The Attorney General is authorized to grant, and shall establish and publish procedures to govern the issuance of, waivers from any requirements under this section to additional categories of advanced technological false personation records upon petition of any producer thereof if such producer can demonstrate that compliance with this section would impede their ability to engage in lawful activities protected by the First Amendment of the Constitution.

"(3) DIGITAL CONTENT PROVENANCE STANDARDS.—Not later than 1 year after the date of enactment of this section, the Attorney General shall issue rules governing the technical specifications of the digital content provenance required under subsection (b) which stall include, if such is determined appropriate, a requirement for such digital content provenance to contain embedded or linked metadata.

"(l) VENUE.—Any action under this section may be brought, in addition to in any district otherwise described in section 1391 of title 28, in the district where or the person falsely depicted in the advanced technological false personation record resides.

"(m) EXTRATERRITORIALITY.—There is extraterritorial Federal jurisdiction over an offense under this section if the defendant or the depicted person is a citizen or permanent resident of the United States.

"(n) DEFINITIONS.—

"(1) ADVANCED TECHNOLOGICAL FALSE PERSONATION RECORD.—The term 'advanced technological false personation record' means any deepfake, which—

"(A) a reasonable person, having considered the visual or audio qualities of the record and the nature of the distribution channel in which the record appears, would believe accurately exhibits—

"(i) any material activity of a living person which such living person did not in fact undertake; or "(ii) any material activity of a deceased person which such deceased person did not in fact undertake, and the exhibition of which is substantially likely to either further a criminal act or result in improper interference in an official proceeding, a public policy debate, or an election; and

"(B) was produced without the consent of such living person, or in the case of a deceased person, such person or the heirs thereof.

"(2) MATERIAL ACTIVITY.—The term 'material activity' means any speech, conduct, or depiction which causes, or a reasonable person would recognize has a tendency to cause perceptible individual or societal harm, including misrepresentation, reputational damage, embarrassment, harassment, financial losses, the incitement of violence, the alteration of a public policy debate or election, or the furtherance of any unlawful act.

"(3) DEEPFAKE.—The term 'deepfake' means any video recording, motion-picture film, sound recording, electronic image, or photograph, or any technological representation of speech or conduct substantially derivative thereof—"(A) which appears to authentically depict any speech or conduct of a person who did not in fact engage in such speech or conduct; and "(B) the production of which was substantially dependent upon technical means, rather than the ability of another person to physically or verbally impersonate such person.

"(o) REPORTS.—The Attorney General, in coordination with other relevant Federal agencies, shall submit a report to Congress 5 years after the date of enactment of this section, and 5 years thereafter, describing trends related to prosecutions and civil penalties pursued under this section.

"§ 1042. DEEPFAKES VICTIM ASSISTANCE

"(a) COORDINATOR FOR VIOLATIONS DIRECTED BY FOREIGN NATION-STATES.—The Attorney General shall designate a coordinator in each United States Attorney's Office to receive reports from the public regarding potential violations of section 1041 relating to deepfake depictions produced or distributed by any foreign nation-state, or any agent acting on its behalf, and coordinate prosecutions for any such violation.

"(b) COORDINATOR FOR FALSE INTIMATE DEPICTIONS.—The Attorney General shall designate a coordinator in each United States Attorney's Office to receive reports from the public regarding potential violations of section 1041 relating to deepfake depictions of an intimate and sexual nature, and coordinate prosecutions for any such violation.

"(c) PLAN AND GUIDANCE.—On the effective date of this section, the Attorney General shall publish a report containing—

"(1) a plan to effectuate and enforce section 1041;

"(2) a description of the efforts of the Russian Federation and the People's Republic of China, and such other states or groups as the Attorney General determines appropriate, to use deepfake technology to impact elections or public policy debates in the United States or other democracies;

"(3) a description of the impact of intimate and sexual deepfakes on women and marginalized communities; and

"(4) in order to increase the likelihood of such prosecutions, official guidance to Federal prosecutors regarding any potential legal concerns that may impede such prosecutions absent clarification.".

(b) CLERICAL AMENDMENT.—The table of sections for chapter 47 of title 18, United States Code, is amended by adding at the end the following:

“1041. Advanced technological false personation record. “1042. Deepfakes victim assistance.”.

SEC. 3. TRANSPARENCY FACILITATION.

(a) IN GENERAL.—Any person who, in or affecting interstate or foreign commerce, for commercial purposes, develops a product that such person reasonably believes, in the context of the intended distribution of the product, will be used to produce deepfakes, as such term is defined in section 1041 of title 18, United States Code, as added by this Act, shall—

(1) ensure such product has the technical capability to insert digital content provenance and disclosures of the nature described in such section into such deepfakes; and

(2) include terms of use or other analogous disclosures with such product, which require the user of such product to affirmatively acknowledge their genral awareness of their legal obligations under section 1041 of title 18, United States Code.

(b) ENFORCEMENT BY FEDERAL TRADE COMMISSION.—

(1) UNFAIR OR DECEPTIVE ACTS OR PRACTICES.—A violation of this section or a regulation promulgated under this section shall be treated as a violation of a regulation under section 18(a)(1)(B) of the Federal Trade Commission Act (15 U.S.C. 57a(a)(1)(B)) regarding unfair or deceptive acts or practices.

(2) POWERS OF COMMISSION.—The Federal Trade Commission shall enforce this section and the regulations promulgated under this section in the same manner, by the same means, and with the same jurisdiction, powers, and duties as though all applicable terms and provisions of the Federal Trade Commission Act (15 U.S.C. 41 et seq.) were incorporated into and made a part of this section. Any person who violates this section or a regulation promulgated under this section shall be subject to the penalties and entitled to the privileges and immunities provided in the Federal Trade Commission Act.

(3) RULEMAKING.—The Federal Trade Commission may promulgate regulations, in accordance with section 553 of title 5, United States Code, to implement this section.

SEC. 4. IN REM LITIGATION AGAINST FOREIGN AND UNKNOWN DEFENDANTS.

(a) IN GENERAL.—A living person, or an affiliated corporate or other entity substantially connected to such living person, exhibited as engaging in falsified material activity in an advanced technological false personation record (as such term is defined in section 1041 of title 18, United States Code), and subject to the exceptions under section 1041(j) of such title, may file an in rem civil action against an advanced technological false personation record, in the judicial district in which such living person or related entity resides, if—

(1) the producer of such advanced technological false personation record is in violation of any provision in section 1041 of title 18, United States Code, for which a private remedy is provided; and

(2) the court finds that such living person or related entity—

(A) is not able to obtain in personam jurisdiction over a person who would have been a defendant in a civil action in section 1041 of title 18, United States Code, as added by section 2 of this Act; or

(B) through reasonable due diligence was not able to find a person who would have been a defendant in a civil action under paragraph

(1) by—

(i) if practicable, sending a notice of the alleged violation and intent to proceed under this paragraph to the producer of the record;

(ii) publishing notice of the action as the court may direct promptly after filing the action; and

(iii) complying with such other due diligence measures the Attorney General promulgates through regulation.

(b) SERVICE OF PROCESS.—The actions under subsection (a)(2)(B)(ii) shall constitute service of process.

(c) JURISDICTION.—In an in rem action under this section, an advanced false personation record shall be deemed to have its situs in the judicial district in which the person falsely depicted as engaging in material activity resides.

(d) REMEDIES.—The remedies in an in rem action under this section shall be limited to—

(1) a court order declaring there to be a substantial likelihood that the material activity depicted in such advanced technological false personation record is false and lacking the digital content provenance and disclosures required under section 1041 of title 18, United States Code, as added by section 2 of this Act; and

(2) as appropriate at the discretion of the court, the forfeiture by the producer of such advanced technological false personation record of profits directly derived from the production and distribution of such record.

(e) ESTOPPEL AND ADDITIONAL REMEDIES.—A court order under subsection (d) may not be used for purposes of estoppel in subsequent litigation should the living person or related entity bringing suit file additional actions under other provisions of law. The in rem action established under this

Act shall be in addition to any other civil action or remedy otherwise applicable and any other jurisdiction that otherwise exists, whether in rem or in personam.

SEC. 5. FRAUD AND RELATED ACTIVITY IN CONNECTION WITH AUDIOVISUAL AND BIOMETRIC IDENTITY AUTHENTICATION.

(a) OFFENSE.—Section 1028 of title 18, United States Code, is amended—

(1) in subsection (a)—

(A) in paragraph (1), by striking "or a false identification document" and inserting "a false identification document, or a false audiovisual identification record";

(B) in paragraph (4), by striking "or a false identification document," and inserting "a false identification document, or a false audio-visual identification record,"; and

(C) in paragraph (5), by striking "a false identification document" and inserting "a false identification document, false audiovisual identification record";

(2) in subsection (b)(1)(A), by striking "or false identification document" and inserting "a false identification document, or a false audiovisual identification record";

(3) in subsection (c)(3)(A), by inserting after "a document" the following: "or a false audiovisual identification record"; and

(4) in subsection (d)—

(A) in paragraph (1), insert after "letters," the following: "biometric indicators";

(B) in paragraph (7), insert after "other unique physical representation" the following:

"including facial dimensions or characteristics, or visual imagery or content which appears to authentically depict any speech or conduct of a person who did not in fact engage in such speech or conduct";

(C) in paragraph (11), strike "and" at the end;

(D) in paragraph (12)(B), strike the period at the end and insert "; and"; and (E) by adding at the end the following:

"(13) The term 'false audiovisual identification record' means any advanced technological false personation record (as such term is defined in section 1041)—

"(A) used or attempted to be used by a person for the purpose of assuming the identity of the person depicted in the advanced technological false personation record without such other person's consent; and

"(B)(i) the use or attempted use of which is intended to further any unlawful activity that constitutes a violation of Federal law, or that constitutes a felony under any applicable State, territorial, or local law;

"(ii) depicts obscenity or sexually explicit conduct, considering the extent to which the record appeals to the prurient interest, is patently offensive, and lacks serious literary, artistic, political, or scientific value;

"(iii) depicts fighting words, which by their very utterance, inflict injury or tend to incite an immediate breach of the peace;

"(iv) constitutes a call to imminent lawless action, and is likely, whether on its own or collectively in connection with related records, to incite or produce such action; or

"(v) depicts or constitutes other activities or speech that the Attorney General determines by regulation pose a credible threat to the national interests of the United States, which, as of the date of such regulation, have been determined by a Federal court to constitute an unprotected class of speech under the first amendment.".

(b) RULE OF CONSTRUCTION.—The amendments made by subsection (a) may not be interpreted as imposing any limitations on the applicability of section 1028 of title 18, United States Code, to any item which was covered by such section prior to the date of enactment of this Act.

SEC. 6. FALSE PERSONATION.

(a) IN GENERAL.—Chapter 43 of title 18 of the United States Code is amended by adding at the end a new section as follows:

"§ 918. DEEPFAKE FALSE PERSONATION GENERALLY

"Section 911 through 917 of this chapter shall be interpreted to include producers, or persons who substantially and knowingly contribute to the production and unlawful use of, advanced technological false personation records (as such term is defined in section 1041), subject to the exceptions under section 4041(j).".

(b) CLERICAL AMENDMENT.—The table of sections for chapter 43 of title 18, United States Code, is amended by adding at the end the following:

"918. Deepfake false personation generally.".

SEC. 7. DETECTION OF DEEPFAKES.

(a) ESTABLISHMENT OF TASK FORCE.—The Secretary of Homeland Security, in coordination with the heads of other relevant Federal entities, shall establish a task force within the Science and Technology

Directorate of the Department of Homeland Security (in this section referred to as the "Deepfakes Task Force"), to—

(1) advance efforts of the United States Government to combat the national security implications of deepfakes;

(2) as appropriate, research and develop technologies to detect, or otherwise counter and combat, deepfakes and other advanced image manipulation methods and distinguish such deepfakes or related forgeries from legitimate audiovisual recordings or visual depictions of actual events;

(3) provide support, both administrative and scientific, to other Federal entities researching such technologies;

(4) encourage efforts of the United States Government to adopt such technologies; and

(5) facilitate discussion and appropriate cooperation between the United States Government and relevant private sector technology enterprises or other nongovernmental entities, including academic and research institutions, regarding the identification of deepfakes or other advanced image manipulation methods.

(b) PRIVATE SECTOR COLLABORATION.—If the United States Government develops technologies to reliably detect deepfakes and other advanced image manipulation methods and distinguish such deepfakes or related forgeries from legitimate audiovisual recordings or visual depictions of actual events, the President shall, unless the President determines such is contrary to the national interests of the United States, seek to make such technologies available to appropriate United States private sector internet platforms, including social networks.

(c) ANNUAL REPORT.—Not later than one year after the date of the enactment of this Act and annually thereafter for five years, the Secretary of Homeland Security shall submit to the Committee on Homeland Security of the House of Representatives and the Committee on Homeland Security and Governmental Affairs of the Senate an unclassified report, which may contain a classified annex, describing the following:

(1) The activities of the Deepfakes Task Force.

(2) As appropriate, technological progress related to the detection of deepfakes and other advanced image manipulation methods.

(3) New developments related to the national security threat posed by deepfakes and other advanced image manipulation methods, which shall include a description of any efforts of the Russian Federation and the People's Republic of China, and such other countries or groups as the Secretary

determines appropriate, to distribute deepfakes or related forgeries in the United States or other democracies.

(4) Related efforts of the United States to combat and counter deepfakes and other advanced image manipulation methods.

(d) DEFINITION.—The term "deepfake" shall have the meaning given such term in section 1041 of title 18, United States Code, as added by section 2 of this Act.

SEC. 8. CONGRESSIONAL NOTIFICATION.

The Secretary of Homeland Security shall annually submit to the Committee on Homeland Security of the House of Representatives and the Committee on Homeland Security and Governmental Affairs of the Senate a classified written notification and, upon request, a briefing, regarding any known attempts of foreign countries to use deepfakes (as such term is defined in section 1041 of title 18, United States Code, as added by section 2 of this Act) or other advanced image manipulation methods to influence or otherwise interfere in an official proceeding within the United States, including an election.

SEC. 9. INFORMATION SHARING.

The Secretary of Homeland Security shall take such actions as may be necessary to establish in the Department of Homeland Security an information sharing program relating to deepfakes (as such term is defined in section 1041 of title 18, United States Code, as added by section 2 of this Act) and other advanced image manipulation methods to permit online platforms (as defined in section 10(d) of this Act) to alert other such platforms to prevent the spread of a malicious deepfake or other related forgery, as well as to promptly alert for public dissemination news organizations regarding such deepfake or related forgery.

SEC. 10. REQUIREMENTS FOR ONLINE PLATFORMS.

(a) TECHNICAL CAPABILITY RELATING TO DIGITAL CONTENT PROVENANCE.—A provider of an online platform shall ensure such platform has the technical capability to insert digital content provenance and disclosures of the nature described in section 1041 of title 18, United States Code, as added by this Act, into any deepfakes that are distributed on such platform.

(b) SYSTEM TO DETECT DEEPFAKES.—A provider of an online platform shall have in place a system to detect deepfakes in the content distributed on such platform.

(c) ENFORCEMENT BY FEDERAL TRADE COMMISSION.—

(1) UNFAIR OR DECEPTIVE ACTS OR PRACTICES.—A violation of this section or a regulation promulgated under this section shall be treated as a violation of a regulation under section 18(a)(1)(B) of the Federal Trade Commission Act (15 U.S.C.57a(a)(1)(B)) regarding unfair or deceptive acts or practices.

(2) POWERS OF COMMISSION.—The Federal Trade Commission shall enforce this section and the regulations promulgated under this section in the same manner, by the same means, and with the same jurisdiction, powers, and duties as though all applicable terms and provisions of the Federal Trade Commission Act (15 U.S.C. 41 et seq.) were incorporated into and made a part of this section. Any person who violates this section or a regulation promulgated under this section shall be subject to the penalties and entitled to the privileges and immunities provided in the Federal Trade Commission Act.

(3) RULEMAKING.—The Federal Trade Commission may promulgate regulations, in accordance with section 553 of title 5, United States Code, to implement this section.

(d) DEFINITIONS.—In this section:

(1) DEEPFAKE.—The term "deepfake" has the meaning given such term in section 1041 of title 18, United States Code, as added by this Act.

(2) ONLINE PLATFORM.—The term "online platform" means any public-facing website, online service, online application, or mobile application which is operated for commercial purposes and provides a community forum for user-generated content, including a social network site, content aggregation service, or service for sharing videos, images, games, audio files, or other content.

SEC. 11. EFFECTIVE DATE.

This Act and the amendments made by this Act shall take effect on the date that is one year after the date of enactment of this Act.

Chapter 4

Deep Fakes and National Security*

Laurie A. Harris

Deep fakes"—a term that first emerged in 2017 to describe realistic photo, audio, video, and other forgeries generated with artificial intelligence (AI) technologies—could present a variety of national security challenges in the years to come. As these technologies continue to mature, they could hold significant implications for congressional oversight, U.S. defense authorizations and appropriations, and the regulation of social media platforms.

How Are Deep Fakes Created?

Though definitions vary, deep fakes are most commonly described as forgeries created using techniques in machine learning (ML)—a subfield of AI—especially generative adversarial networks (GANs). In the GAN process, two ML systems called neural networks are trained in competition with each other. The first network, or the generator, is tasked with creating counterfeit data—such as photos, audio recordings, or video footage—that replicate the properties of the original data set. The second network, or the discriminator, is tasked with identifying the counterfeit data. Based on the results of each iteration, the generator network adjusts to create increasingly realistic data. The networks continue to compete—often for thousands or millions of iterations—until the generator improves its performance such that the discriminator can no longer distinguish between real and counterfeit data.

* This is an edited, reformatted and augmented version of Congressional Research Service Publication No. IF11333, updated April 17, 2023.

In: The Deepfake Dilemma
Editor: Ruben Faulkner
ISBN: 979-8-90134-122-3

Though media manipulation is not a new phenomenon, the use of AI to generate deep fakes is causing concern because the results are increasingly realistic, rapidly created, and cheaply made with freely available software and the ability to rent processing power through cloud computing. Thus, even unskilled operators could download the requisite software tools and, using publically available data, create increasingly convincing counterfeit content.

How Could Deep Fakes Be Used?

Deep fake technology has been popularized for entertainment purposes—for example, social media users inserting the actor Nicholas Cage into movies in which he did not originally appear and a museum generating an interactive exhibit with artist Salvador Dalí. Deep fake technologies have also been used for beneficial purposes. For example, medical researchers have reported using GANs to synthesize fake medical images to train disease detection algorithms for rare diseases and to minimize patient privacy concerns.

Deep fakes could, however, be used for nefarious purposes. State adversaries or politically motivated individuals could release falsified videos of elected officials or other public figures making incendiary comments or behaving inappropriately. Doing so could, in turn, erode public trust, negatively affect public discourse, or even sway an election.

Indeed, the U.S. intelligence community concluded that Russia engaged in extensive influence operations during the 2016 presidential election to "undermine public faith in the U.S. democratic process, denigrate Secretary Clinton, and harm her electability and potential presidency." Likewise, in March 2022, Ukrainian President Volodymyr Zelensky announced that a video posted to social media—in which he appeared to direct Ukrainian soldiers to surrender to Russian forces—was a deep fake. While experts noted that this deep fake was not particularly sophisticated, in the future, convincing audio or video forgeries could potentially strengthen malicious influence operations.

Deep fakes could also be used to embarrass or blackmail elected officials or individuals with access to classified information. Already there is evidence that foreign intelligence operatives have used deep fake photos to create fake social media accounts from which they have attempted to recruit sources. Some analysts have suggested that deep fakes could similarly be used to generate inflammatory content—such as convincing video of U.S. military personnel engaged in war crimes—intended to radicalize populations, recruit terrorists, or incite violence. Section 589F of the FY2021 National Defense Authorization Act (P.L. 116-283) directs the Secretary of Defense to conduct an intelligence assessment of the threat posed by deep fakes to servicemembers and their families, including an assessment of the maturity of the technology and how it might be used to conduct information operations.

In addition, deep fakes could produce an effect that professors Danielle Keats Citron and Robert Chesney have termed the "Liar's Dividend"; it involves the notion that individuals could successfully deny the authenticity of genuine content—particularly if it depicts inappropriate or criminal behavior—by claiming that the content is a deep fake. Citron and Chesney suggest that the Liar's Dividend could become more powerful as deep fake technology proliferates and public knowledge of the technology grows.

Some reports indicate that such tactics have already been used for political purposes. For example, political opponents of Gabon President Ali Bongo asserted that a video intended to demonstrate his good health and mental competency was a deep fake, later citing it as part of the justification for an attempted coup. Outside experts were unable to determine the video's authenticity, but one expert noted, "in some ways it doesn't matter if [the video is] a fake… It can be used to just undermine credibility and cast doubt."

How Can Deep Fakes Be Detected?

Today, deep fakes can often be detected without specialized detection tools. However, the sophistication of the technology is rapidly progressing to a point at which unaided human detection will be very difficult or impossible. While commercial industry has been investing in automated deep fake detection tools, this section describes U.S. government investments and activities.

The Identifying Outputs of Generative Adversarial Networks Act (P.L. 116-258) directed NSF and NIST to support research on GANs. Specifically, NSF is directed to support research on manipulated or synthesized content and information authenticity, and NIST is directed to support research for the development of measurements and standards necessary to develop tools to examine the function and outputs of GANs or other technologies that synthesize or manipulate content.

In addition, DARPA has had two programs devoted to the detection of deep fakes: Media Forensics (MediFor) and Semantic Forensics (SemaFor). MediFor, which concluded in FY2021, was to develop algorithms to automatically assess the integrity of photos and videos and to provide analysts with information about how counterfeit content was generated. The program reportedly explored techniques for identifying the audio-visual inconsistencies present in deep fakes, including inconsistencies in pixels (digital integrity), inconsistencies with the laws of physics (physical integrity), and inconsistencies with other information sources (semantic integrity). MediFor technologies are expected to transition to operational commands and the intelligence community.

SemaFor seeks to build upon MediFor technologies and to develop algorithms that will automatically detect, attribute, and characterize (i.e., identify as either benign or malicious) various types of deep fakes. This program is to catalog semantic inconsistencies—such as the mismatched earrings seen in the GAN-generated image in Figure 1, or unusual facial features or backgrounds—and prioritize suspected deep fakes for human review. DARPA requested $18 million for SemaFor in FY2024, $4 million under the FY2023 appropriation. Technologies developed by both SemaFor and MediFor are intended to improve defenses against adversary information operations.

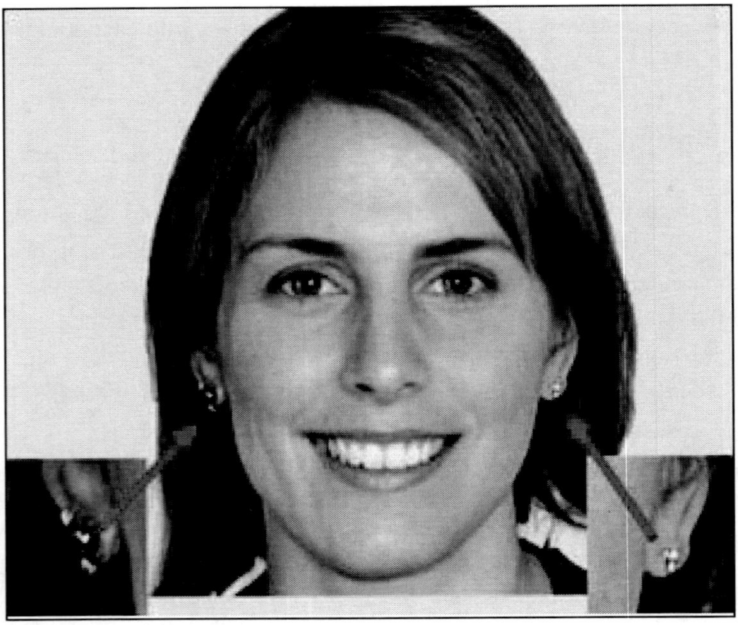

Source: https://www.darpa.mil/news-events/2019-09-03a.

Figure 1. Example of Semantic Inconsistency in a GAN-Generated Image.

Policy Considerations

Some analysts have noted that algorithm-based detection tools could lead to a cat-and-mouse game, in which the deep fake generators are rapidly updated to address flaws identified by detection tools. For this reason, they argue that social media platforms—in addition to deploying deep fake detection tools—may need to expand the means of labeling and/or authenticating content. This could include a requirement that users identify the time and location at which the content originated or that they label edited content as such.

Other analysts have expressed concern that regulation of deep fake technology could impose undue burden on social media platforms or lead to unconstitutional restrictions on free speech and artistic expression. These analysts have suggested that existing law is sufficient for managing the malicious use of deep fakes. Some experts have asserted that responding with technical tools alone will be insufficient and that instead the focus should be on the need to educate the public about deep fakes and minimize incentives for creators of malicious deep fakes.

Potential Questions for Congress

- Do the Department of Defense, the Department of State, and the intelligence community have adequate information about the state of foreign deep fake technology and the ways in which this technology may be used to harm U.S. national security?
- How mature are DARPA's efforts to develop automated deep fake detection tools? What are the limitations of DARPA's approach, and are any additional efforts required to ensure that malicious deep fakes do not harm U.S. national security?
- Are federal investments and coordination efforts, across defense and nondefense agencies and with the private sector, adequate to address research and development needs and national security concerns regarding deep fake technologies?
- How should national security considerations with regard to deep fakes be balanced with free speech protections, artistic expression, and beneficial uses of the underlying technologies?
- Should social media platforms be required to authenticate or label content? Should users be required to submit information about the

provenance of content? What secondary effects could this have for social media platforms and the safety, security, and privacy of users?

- To what extent and in what manner, if at all, should social media platforms and users be held accountable for the dissemination and impacts of malicious deep fake content?
- What efforts, if any, should the U.S. government undertake to ensure that the public is educated about deep fakes?

CRS Products

CRS Report R46795, Artificial Intelligence: Background, Selected Issues, and Policy Considerations, by Laurie A. Harris

CRS Report R45178, Artificial Intelligence and National Security, by Kelley M. Sayler

CRS Report R45142, Information Warfare: Issues for Congress, by Catherine A. Theohary

Chapter 5

Combating Deepfakes*

U.S. Government Accountability Office

Why This Matters

Malicious use of deepfakes could erode trust in elections, spread disinformation, undermine national security, and empower harassers.

Key Takeaways

- Current deepfake detection technologies have limited effectiveness in real-world scenarios.
- Watermarking and other authentication technologies may slow the spread of disinformation but present challenges.
- Identifying deepfakes is not by itself sufficient to prevent abuses. It may not stop the spread of disinformation, even after the media is identified as a deepfake.

* This is an edited, reformatted and augmented version of the United States Government Accountability Office Report, Publication No. GAO-24-107292, dated March, 2024.

In: The Deepfake Dilemma
Editor: Ruben Faulkner
ISBN: 979-8-90134-122-3

The Technology

What is It?

Deepfakes are videos, audio, or images that have been manipulated using artificial intelligence (AI), often to create, replace, or alter faces or synthesize speech. They can seem authentic to the human eye and ear. They have been maliciously used, for example, to try to influence elections and to create non-consensual pornography. To combat such abuses, technologies can be used to detect deepfakes or enable authentication of genuine media.

Detection technologies aim to identify fake media without needing to compare it to the original, unaltered media. These technologies typically use a form of AI known as machine learning. The models are trained on data from known real and fake media. Methods include looking for (1) facial or vocal inconsistencies, (2) evidence of the deepfake generation process, or (3) color abnormalities.

Authentication technologies are designed to be embedded during the creation of a piece of media. These technologies aim to either prove authenticity or prove that a specific original piece of media has been altered. They include:

- *Digital watermarks* can be embedded in a piece of media, which can help detect subsequent deepfakes. One form of watermarking adds pixel or audio patterns that are detectable by a computer but are imperceptible to humans. The patterns disappear in any areas that are modified, enabling the owner to prove that the media is an altered version of the original. Another form of watermarking adds features that cause any deepfake made using the media to look or sound unrealistic.
- *Metadata*—which describe the characteristics of data in a piece of media—can be embedded in a way that is cryptographically secure. Missing or incomplete metadata may indicate that a piece of media has been altered.
- *Blockchain.* Uploading media and metadata to a public blockchain creates a relatively secure version that cannot be altered without the change being obvious to other users. Anyone could then compare a file and its metadata to the blockchain version to prove or disprove authenticity.

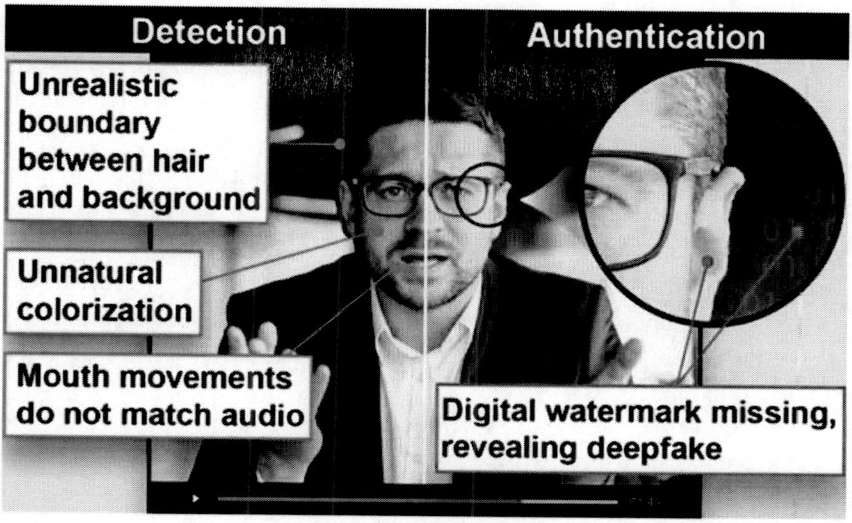

Sources: GAO analysis (data); Tetiana/sanchesnet1/stock.adobe.com (images). | GAO-24-107292

Figure 1. Examples of Deepfake Detection and Authentication.

How Mature Is It?

Detection technologies. According to recent studies, existing detection methods and models may not accurately identify deepfakes in real-world scenarios. For example, accuracy may be reduced if lighting conditions, facial expressions, or video or audio quality are different from the data used to train the detection model, or if the deepfake was created using a different method than that used in the training data. Further, future advances in deepfake generation are expected to eliminate hallmarks of current deepfakes, such as abnormal eye blinking.

Authentication technologies. These technologies are not new, but their use in combating deepfakes is an emerging area.

Several companies offer authentication services, including using digital watermarks, metadata, and blockchain technologies.

Some claim to let website visitors authenticate media found on the internet, provided the original is in the company's database. Prominent social media companies are also beginning to label AI-generated content.

Opportunities

- *Combined defenses.* Using multiple detection and authentication methods may help to identify deepfakes.
- *Updated training datasets.* Including diverse and recent media in training data could help detection models keep up with the latest deepfake generation techniques.
- *Competitions.* Deepfake detection competitions could encourage the development of more accurate detection tools and models. One 2019 competition included over 2,000 participants and generated over 35,000 models.

Challenges

- Disinformation and public trust. Disinformation can spread from the moment a deepfake is viewed, even if it is identified as fraudulent. Further, trust in real media may be undermined by false claims that real media is a deepfake or if people do not trust a detection model's results.
- Adaptation to detection. Techniques and models used to identify deepfakes tend to lead developers to create more sophisticated deepfake generation techniques.

Policy Context and Questions

- Are current laws and regulations adequate to address evolving concerns about the malicious use of deepfakes? How do they address data security, privacy concerns, and First Amendment considerations, such as a deepfake creator's freedom of speech and expression?
- What entities (e.g., government, nonprofit, private company) should make decisions about identifying and blocking deepfakes, or about when and how to sanction those who produce or disseminate them?
- How can organizations across society coordinate on the development and improvement of deepfake detection and authentication technologies? What standards could be used or developed to evaluate these technologies?

Selected GAO Work

Science & Tech Spotlight: Deepfakes,
GAO-20-379SP Technology Assessment: Blockchain, GAO-22-104625

Selected References

Gourav Gupta, Kiran Raja, Manish Gupta, Tony Jan, Scott Thompson Whiteside, and Mukesh Prasad, "A Comprehensive Review of DeepFake Detection Using Advanced Machine Learning and Fusion Methods," *Electronics*, vol. 13, no. 95 (2024) https://doi.org/10.3390/electronics13010095.

National Security Agency, Federal Bureau of Investigation, and Cybersecurity and Infrastructure Security Agency, *Contextualizing Deepfake Threats to Organizations*, Sept. 2023.

Gao Support

The Government Accountability Office (GAO) meets congressional information needs in several ways, including by providing oversight, insight, and foresight on science and technology issues. GAO staff are available to brief on completed bodies of work or specific reports and answer follow- up questions. GAO also provides targeted assistance on specific science and technology topics to support congressional oversight activities and provide advice on legislative proposals.

For more information, contact: Brian Bothwell at (202) 512-6888 or bothwellb@gao.gov.

Congressional Relations: A. Nicole Clowers, Managing Dir., (202) 512-4400, clowersa@gao.gov.

Public Affairs: Charles Young, Managing Dir., (202) 512-4800, youngc1@gao.gov.

This document is not an audit product and is subject to revision based on continued advances in science and technology. It contains information prepared by GAO to provide technical insight to legislative bodies or other external organizations. This document has been reviewed by Sterling Thomas, PhD, the Chief Scientist of the U.S. Government Accountability Office.

Staff Acknowledgments: Laura Holliday (Assistant Director), Douglas G. Hunker (Analyst-in- Charge), Shannon Brooks, Nirmal Chaudhary, Caroline Gross, Anika McMillon, and Benjamin Shouse.

Source: Debalina/stock.adobe.com (header). | GAO-24-107292.

Chapter 6

Tools to Address Known Exploitation by Immobilizing Technological Deepfakes on Websites and Networks Act*

Committee on Energy and Commerce

The Committee on Energy and Commerce, to whom was referred the bill (H.R. 633) to require covered platforms to remove non-consensual intimate visual depictions, and for other purposes, having considered the same, reports favorably thereon without amendment and recommends that the bill do pass.

Purpose and Summary

H.R. 633, the Tools to Address Known Exploitation by Immobilizing Technological Deepfakes on Websites and Networks Act, or the TAKE IT DOWN Act, was introduced by Representative Salazar on January 22, 2025, and referred to the Committee on Energy and Commerce. H.R. 633 criminalizes the publication of non-consensual intimate images (NCII) or the threat to publish NCII in interstate commerce. NCII is defined to include realistic, computer-generated pornographic images and videos that depict identifiable, real people. The bill permits the good faith disclosure of NCII, such as disclosure to law enforcement or for medical treatment. The bill requires covered platforms to establish and implement a notice and takedown

* This is an edited, reformatted and augmented version of a Report submitted by Mr. Guthrie from the Committee on Energy and Commerce and Committed to the Committee of the Whole House on the State of the Union and ordered to be printed together with Minority Views, [To accompany H.R. 633], Publication No. 119–82, dated APRIL 28, 2025.

In: The Deepfake Dilemma
Editor: Ruben Faulkner
ISBN: 979-8-90134-122-3

process within one year of enactment. The takedown process requires covered platforms to remove NCII, and known copies of such NCII, within forty-eight hours upon receiving a valid removal request notice from an identifiable individual. The bill provides that a failure to reasonably comply with the notice and take down obligations under the Act shall be treated as a violation of a rule defining an unfair or a deceptive act or practice under Section 18(a)(1)(B) of the Federal Trade Commission Act (15 U.S.C. 41 et seq.).

Background and Need for Legislation

Artificial intelligence (AI) has drastically changed how people interact with computer services. For instance, the availability, and advancement, of AI, and other computer-generated technologies, has improved the way Americans can complete mundane tasks, compile and access information,[1] and assist collaboration between humans in work environments.[2] It also promises to assist law enforcement fight against different types of fraud and abuse.[3] However, the growth and advancement of AI, while benefitting many different avenues of society, can also be used by bad actors to create and distribution of NCII of adults and minors, resulting in significant harm to Americans.

Before the rapid advancement of AI, especially generative AI, NCII depicted real images or videos of actual people.[4] But the rise of the new technology is exposing a hole in protections for Americans, especially children. Bad actors can use AI to create a digital forgery of NCII which involves manipulating real pictures easily obtained from online to falsely depict and expose an individual in intimate situations or in sexually graphic

---

[1] *See* Jerry Patterson, *Ways AI can improve our world*, ROWAN UNIVERSITY INFORMATION RESOURCES & TECHNOLOGY NEWS (last accessed Apr. 9, 2025), https://irt.rowan.edu/about/news/ 2024/10/ai-benefits.html.

[2] *See* Hanae Armitage, *How AI improves physician and nurse collaboration*, STANFORD MEDICINE NEWS CENTER (Apr. 15, 2024) https://med.stanford.edu/news/all-news/2024/04/ai-patient-care.html.

[3] *See* Rabihah Butler, *How AI can help law enforcement fight fraud & other crimes*, THOMSON REUTERS (Sep. 30, 2024) https://www.thomsonreuters.com/en-us/posts/government/ai-law- enforcement-fraud/.

[4] *See* Danielle K. Citron & Mary A. Franks, *Criminalizing Revenge Porn*, UNIV. OF MARYLAND FRANCIS KING SCH. OF L. (May 19, 2024), https://digital commons. law.umaryland.edu/fac_pubs/ 1420/.

manners.[5] Although such digital forgery NCII is not authentic, it harms the real people de picted, including psychological harm such as humiliation, public shaming, and depression, as well as physical harm such as self-harm and suicide.[6] The possibility that these images can continue to be spread—possibly in perpetuity if allowed to remain online— compounds the traumatic impact of those harmed by these images. NCII, including deepfake NCII, is also used by predators to commit sextortion, which involves soliciting and encouraging individuals to record or photograph themselves engaged in sexual acts or scenarios. In some cases, the predator may not already have a revealing picture or video recording, and at the first point of contact they will threaten an individual as if they did have sexually revealing information to obtain more sexually explicit images or recordings.[7] Once a predator has recordings or images they will exploit or blackmail the victim for money or additional favors by threatening to publicly release any of the recordings or photographs of the victim.[8]

NCII, real or AI generated, has contributed life long lasting harms to Americans throughout the United States, but particularly our children. Furthermore, there are few remedies victims may utilize to protect themselves. On March 26, 2025, the Committee on Energy and Commerce held a hearing which highlighted the lack of legal remedies available to law enforcement to pursue predators and culprits taking advantage of children.[9] The hearing also demonstrated how difficult it is for victims to remove any real or AI generated NCII from online platforms.[10]

---

[5] *See* Karen Hao, *Deepfake Porn is Ruining Women's Lives. Now the Law May Finally Ban It*, MASS. INST. TECH. TECH. REV. (Feb. 12, 2021), https://www.technologyreview.com/2021/02/12/ 1018222/deepfake-revenge-porn-coming-ban/.

[6] *See* Richard Jochelson et al, *Clearing Your History: A Review of Non-Consensual Distribution of Intimate Images in Canada and Future Responses*, 54(3):771 UBC LAW REVIEW (2021). https://commons.allard.ubc.ca/cgi/viewcontent.cgi?article=1014&context=ubclawreview.

[7] *See* Federal Bureau of Investigation (FBI), *How We Can Help You, Scams and Safety, Sextortion*, FBI (last accessed on Apr. 9, 2025) https://www.fbi.gov/how-we-can-help-you/scams- and-safety/common-frauds-and-scams/sextortion.

[8] *See* Elizabeth Clement-Webb, *Sextortion: A Growing Threat Targeting Minors*, FBI (January 23, 2024) https://www.fbi.gov/contact-us/field-offices/nashville/news/sextortion-a-growing-threat- targeting-minors; FBI, *Malicious Actors Manipulating Photos and Videos to Create Explicit Content and Sextortion Schemes* (Jun. 5, 2023) https://www.ic3.gov/PSA/2023/psa230605.

[9] *The World Wild Web: Examining Harms Online: Hearing Before the H. Subcomm. on Commerce, Manufacturing, and Trade, Comm. on Energy and Commerce*, 119th Cong. (2025).

[10] *Id.*

To protect Americans, including our most vulnerable population—children—it is imperative Congress legislate to provide law enforcement with new authorities to address the growing crisis of NCII. Congress must also provide Americans with additional tools to request that NCII be taken down from online platforms by requiring notice and take down obligations for entities where NCII is found. H.R. 633 clarifies that the creation and publication of NCII in interstate commerce, or the threat to publish NCII, is a criminal offense in the United States and requires online platforms institute a notice and takedown process enforced by the Federal Trade Commission.

Committee Action

On March 26, 2025, the Subcommittee on Commerce, Manufacturing, and Trade held a hearing titled, "The World Wild Web: Examining Harms Online." The Subcommittee received testimony from:

- Dawn Hawkins, Senior Advisor, National Center on Sexual Exploitation;
- Yiota Souras, Chief Legal Officer, National Center for Missing and Exploited Children;
- Clare Morell, Fellow, Ethics and Public Policy Center; and
- The Honorable Rebecca Kelly Slaughter, Former Commissioner, Federal Trade Commission.

On April 8, 2025, the full Committee on Energy and Commerce met in open markup session and ordered H.R. 633, without amendment, favorably reported to the House by a record vote of 49 yeas and 1 nay.

Committee Votes

Clause 3(b) of rule XIII requires the Committee to list the record votes on the motion to report legislation and amendments thereto. The following reflects the record votes taken during the Committee consideration:

As of 02/24/2025

COMMITTEE ON ENERGY AND COMMERCE
119TH CONGRESS
ROLL CALL VOTE # 6

BILL: H.R. 633

AMENDMENT: Final Passage

DISPOSITION: **Agreed to,** by a roll call vote of 49 yeas and 1 nays.

REPRESENTATIVE	YEAS	NAYS	PRESENT	REPRESENTATIVE	YEAS	NAYS	PRESENT
Mr. Guthrie	X			Mr. Pallone	X		
Mr. Latta	X			Ms. DeGette	X		
Mr. Griffith	X			Ms. Schakowsky	X		
Mr. Bilirakis	X			Ms. Matsui	X		
Mr. Hudson	X			Ms. Castor	X		
Mr. Carter (GA)	X			Mr. Tonko	X		
Mr. Palmer	X			Ms. Clarke		X	
Mr. Dunn	X			Mr. Ruiz	X		
Mr. Crenshaw	X			Mr. Peters			
Mr. Joyce	X			Mrs. Dingell	X		
Mr. Weber	X			Mr. Veasey	X		
Mr. Allen	X			Ms. Kelly	X		
Mr. Balderson	X			Ms. Barragán	X		
Mr. Fulcher	X			Mr. Soto	X		
Mr. Pfluger	X			Ms. Schrier	X		
Mrs. Harshbarger	X			Ms. Trahan	X		
Mrs. Miller-Meeks	X			Ms. Fletcher	X		
Mrs. Cammack	X			Ms. Ocasio-Cortez	X		
Mr. Obernolte				Mr. Auchincloss	X		
Mr. James	X			Mr. Carter (LA)	X		
Mr. Bentz				Mr. Menendez	X		
Mrs. Houchin	X			Mr. Mullin	X		
Mr. Fry				Mr. Landsman	X		
Ms. Lee	X			Ms. McClellan	X		
Mr. Langworthy	X						
Mr. Kean	X						
Mr. Rulli	X						
Mr. Evans	X						
Mr. Goldman	X						
Mrs. Fedorchak	X						

04/08/2025

__/30 __/24

Oversight Findings and Recommendations

Pursuant to clause 2(b)(1) of rule X and clause 3(c)(1) of rule XIII, the Committee has held hearings and made findings that are reflected in this report.

New Budget Authority, Entitlement Authority, and Tax Expenditures

Pursuant to clause 3(c)(2) of rule XIII, the Committee finds that H.R. 633 would result in no new or increased budget authority, entitlement authority, or tax expenditures or revenues.

Congressional Budget Office Estimate

Pursuant to clause 3(c)(3) of rule XIII, at the time this report was filed, the cost estimate prepared by the Director of the Congressional Budget Office pursuant to section 402 of the Congressional Budget Act of 1974 was not available.

Federal Mandates Statement

The Committee adopts as its own the estimate of Federal mandates prepared by the Director of the Congressional Budget Office pursuant to section 423 of the Unfunded Mandates Reform Act.

Statement of General Performance Goals and Objectives

Pursuant to clause 3(c)(4) of rule XIII, the general performance goal or objective of this legislation is to define criminal penalties for the publication or threatened publication of nonconsensual intimate image and to require online platforms to create and publish a process for giving notice of nonconsensual intimate imagery published on the platform within forty-eight hours.

Duplication of Federal Programs

Pursuant to clause 3(c)(5) of rule XIII, no provision of H.R. 633 is known to be duplicative of another Federal program, including any program that was included in a report to Congress pursuant to section 21 of Public Law 111–139 or the most recent Catalog of Federal Domestic Assistance.

Related Committee and Subcommittee Hearings

Pursuant to clause 3(c)(6) of rule XIII, the following related hearing was used to develop or consider H.R. 633:

- On March 26, 2025, the Subcommittee on Commerce, Manufacturing, and Trade held a hearing entitled "The World Wild Web: Examining Harms Online." The Subcommittee received testimony from:
    - Dawn Hawkins, Senior Advisor, National Center on Sexual Exploitation;
    - Yiota Souras, Chief Legal Officer, National Center for Missing and Exploited Children;
    - Clare Morell, Fellow, Ethics and Public Policy Center; and
    - Rebecca Kelly Slaughter, Former Commissioner, Federal Trade Commission.

Committee Cost Estimate

Pursuant to clause 3(d)(1) of rule XIII, the Committee adopts as its own the cost estimate prepared by the Director of the Congressional Budget Office pursuant to section 402 of the Congressional Budget Act of 1974. At the time this report was filed, the estimate was not available.

Earmark, Limited Tax Benefits, and Limited Tariff Benefits

Pursuant to clause 9(e), 9(f), and 9(g) of rule XXI, the Committee finds that H.R. 633 contains no earmarks, limited tax benefits, or limited tariff benefits.

Advisory Committee Statement

No advisory committees within the meaning of section 5(b) of the Federal Advisory Committee Act were created by this legislation.

Applicability to Legislative Branch

The Committee finds that the legislation does not relate to the terms and conditions of employment or access to public services or accommodations within the meaning of section 102(b)(3) of the Congressional Accountability Act.

Section-by-Section Analysis of the Legislation

Section 1. Short Title

Section 1 designates that the short title may be cited as the "Tools to Address Known Exploitation by Immobilizing Technological Deepfakes on Websites and Networks Act" or the "TAKE IT DOWN Act."

Section 2. Criminal Prohibition on Intentional Disclosure of Non- Consensual Intimate Visual Depictions

Section 2 amends the Communications Act of 1934 (47 U.S.C. 223) to create a new Federal crime for the intentional disclosure of nonconsensual intimate visual depictions. Subsection (a)(2) establishes a new Federal criminal provision that makes it unlawful for a person to use an interactive computer service to knowingly publish or threaten to publish an intimate visual depiction of an identifiable individual and includes penalties. The bill provides two different offenses under subsection (2)(A) and (2)(B) depending on whether the identifiable individual within an intimate visual depiction is of an adult or minor.

Subsection (a)(3) establishes a criminal provision that makes it unlawful for a person to use an interactive computer service to knowingly publish a digital forgery of an identifiable individual. The bill provides two different offenses under 3(A) and 3(B) depending on whether the identifiable individual within an intimate visual depiction is of an adult or a minor. Subsection 3(C) clarifies subsections (A) and (B) do not apply to any law enforcement investigations, or disclosures made in good faith to law enforcement, in legal proceedings, as part of a medical diagnosis, to seek support with respect to receipt.

Section 2 provides for further exceptions and penalties, including for intentional threats to commit an offense under this Section against adults and minors.

Section 3. Notice and Removal of Nonconsensual Intimate Visual Depictions

Section 3 requires covered platforms to establish and implement a notice and takedown process within one year of the enactment of this Act in accordance with the requirements outlined in this Section. Subsection (a)(1)(A) establishes the overall requirements for the covered platform to implement the notice and takedown process, including a process for an identifiable individual to notify the platform of an intimate visual depiction that has been published on the covered platform and the ability to submit a request to remove the intimate visual depiction.

Subsection (a)(3) requires a covered platform, "upon receiving a valid removal request" to use the process described in paragraph (1)(A)(ii) "not later than 48 hours" after receiving such request—(1) remove the intimate visual depiction; and (2) make reasonable efforts to identify and remove any known identical copies of such depiction. Subsection (a)(4) provides a limitation on liability to enable covered platforms to comply with the notice and takedown process without incurring liability for good faith disabling of access to, or removal of, material claimed to be a nonconsensual intimate visual depiction.

Subsection (b)(1) provides that a failure to reasonably comply with the notice and take down obligations under subsection (a) shall be treated as a violation of a rule defining an unfair or a deceptive act or practice under Section 18(a)(1)(B) of the Federal Trade Commission Act.

Section 4. Definitions

Section 4 provides definitions that apply to the entirety of this Act.

The terms "consent", "digital forgery", "identifiable individual", "intimate visual depiction", and "minor" have the meaning given such terms in section 223(h) of the Communications Act of 1934 (47 U.S.C. 223), as added by section 2.

This section defines the term "covered platform" as a website, online service, online application, or mobile application: (i) that serves the public and (I) that primarily provides a forum for user-generated content, including messages, videos, images, games, and audio files; or (II) for which it is in the regular course of trade or business of the website, online service, online application, or mobile application to publish, curate, host, or make available content of nonconsensual intimate visual depictions.

The term "covered platform" does not include: (i) broadband internet access service providers (as described in section 8.1(b) of title 47, Code of Federal Regulations, or successor regulation), (ii) electronic mail, (iii) except for those covered platforms that publish or make available in the regular course of business nonconsensual intimate visual depictions, an online service, application, or website that consists primarily of content that is not user generated but is preselected by the provider of such; and for which any chat, comment, or interactive functionality is incidental to, directly related to, or dependent on providing content.

Section 5. Severability

This section provides that if any provision of this Act or amendment made by the Act is determined to be unenforceable or invalid, all remaining provisions and amendments shall not be affected.

Changes in Existing Law Made by the Bill, as Reported

In compliance with clause 3(e) of rule XIII of the Rules of the House of Representatives, changes in existing law made by the bill, as reported, are shown as follows (existing law proposed to be omitted is enclosed in black brackets, new matter is printed in italics, and existing law in which no change is proposed is shown in roman):

Communications Act of 1934

* * * * * * *

Title II—Common Carriers
Part I—Common Carrier Regulation

* * * * * * *

Sec. 223. Obscene or Harassing Telephone Calls in the District of Columbia or in Interstate or Foreign Communications

(a) Whoever—

(1) in interstate or foreign communications—

(A) by means of a telecommunications device knowingly—

(i) makes, creates, or solicits, and

(ii) initiates the transmission of, any comment, request, suggestion, proposal, image, or other communication which is obscene or child pornography, with intent to annoy, abuse, threaten, or harass another person;

(B) by means of a telecommunications device knowingly—

(i) makes, creates, or solicits, and

(ii) initiates the transmission of, any comment, request, suggestion, proposal, image, or other communication which is obscene or child pornography, knowing that the recipient of the communication is under 18 years of age, regardless of whether the maker of such communication placed the call or initiated the communication; makes a telephone call or utilizes a telecommunications device, whether or not conversation or communication ensues, without disclosing his identity and with intent to annoy, abuse, threaten, or harass any person at the called number or who receives the communications;

(C) makes or causes the telephone of another repeatedly or continuously to ring, with intent to harass any person at the called number; or

(D) makes repeated telephone calls or repeatedly initiates communication with a telecommunications device, during which conversation or communication ensues, solely to harass any person at the called number or who receives the communication; or

(2) knowingly permits any telecommunications facility under his control to be used for any activity prohibited by paragraph

(1) with the intent that it be used for such activity, shall be fined under title 18, United States Code, or imprisoned not more than two years, or both.

(b)(1) Whoever knowingly—

(A) within the United States, by means of telephone, makes (directly or by recording device) any obscene communication for commercial purposes to any person, regardless of whether the maker of such communication placed the call; or

(B) permits any telephone facility under such person's control to be used for an activity prohibited by subparagraph (A), shall be fined in accordance with title 18, United States Code, or imprisoned not more than two years, or both.

(2) Whoever knowingly—within the United States, by means of telephone, makes (directly or by recording device) any indecent communication for commercial purposes which is available to any person under 18 years of age or to any other person without that person's consent, regardless of whether the maker of such communication placed the call; or (B) permits any telephone facility under such person's control to be used for an activity prohibited by subparagraph (A), shall be fined not more than $50,000 or imprisoned not more than six months, or both.

(3) It is a defense to prosecution under paragraph (2) of this subsection that the defendant restricted access to the prohibited communication to persons 18 years of age or older in accordance with subsection (c) of this section and with such procedures as the Commission may prescribe by regulation.

(4) In addition to the penalties under paragraph (1), whoever, within the United States, intentionally violates paragraph (1) or (2) shall be subject to a fine of not more than $50,000 for each violation. For purposes of this paragraph, each day of violation shall constitute a separate violation.

(5)(A) In addition to the penalties under paragraphs (1), (2), and (5), whoever, within the United States, violates paragraph (1) or (2) shall be subject to a civil fine of not more than $50,000 for each violation. For purposes of this paragraph, each day of violation shall constitute a separate violation.

(B) A fine under this paragraph may be assessed either—

(i) by a court, pursuant to civil action by the Commission or any attorney employed by the Commission who is designated by the Commission for such purposes, or by the Commission after appropriate administrative proceedings.

(6) The Attorney General may bring a suit in the appropriate district court of the United States to enjoin any act or practice which violates paragraph (1) or (2). An injunction may be granted in accordance with the Federal Rules of Civil Procedure.

(c)(1) A common carrier within the District of Columbia or within any State, or in interstate or foreign commerce, shall not, to the extent technically feasible, provide access to a communication specified in subsection (b) from the telephone of any subscriber who has not previously requested in writing the carrier to provide access to such communication if the carrier collects from subscribers an identifiable charge for such communication that the carrier remits, in whole or in part, to the provider of such communication.

(2) Except as provided in paragraph (3), no cause of action may be brought in any court or administrative agency against any common carrier, or any of its affiliates, including their officers, directors, employees, agents, or authorized representatives on account of—

(A) any action which the carrier demonstrates was taken in good faith to restrict access pursuant to paragraph (1) of this subsection; or any access permitted—

(i) in good faith reliance upon the lack of any representation by a provider of communications that communications provided by that provider are communications specified in subsection (b), or

(ii) because a specific representation by the provider did not allow the carrier, acting in good faith, a sufficient period to restrict access to communications described in subsection (b).

(3) Notwithstanding paragraph (2) of this subsection, a provider of communications services to which subscribers are denied access pursuant to paragraph (1) of this subsection may bring an action for a declaratory judgment or similar action in a court. Any such action shall be limited to the question of whether the communications which the provider seeks to provide fall within the category of communications to which the carrier will provide access only to subscribers who have previously requested such access.

(d) Whoever—

in interstate or foreign communications knowingly—(A) uses an interactive computer service to send to a specific person or persons under 18 years of age, or

(B) uses any interactive computer service to display in a manner available to a person under 18 years of age, any comment, request, suggestion, proposal, image, or other communication that is obscene or child pornography, regardless of whether the user of such service placed the call or initiated the communication; or

(2) knowingly permits any telecommunications facility under such person's control to be used for an activity prohibited by paragraph (1) with the intent that it be used for such activity, shall be fined under title 18, United States Code, or imprisoned not more than two years, or both.

(e) In addition to any other defenses available by law:

(1) No person shall be held to have violated subsection

(a) øor (d)¿, *(d), or (h)* solely for providing access or connection to or from a facility, system, or network not under that person's control, including transmission, downloading, intermediate storage, access software, or other related capabilities that are incidental to providing such access or connection that does not include the creation of the content of the communication.

(1) The defenses provided by paragraph (1) of this subsection shall not be applicable to a person who is a conspirator with an entity actively involved in the creation or knowing distribution of communications that violate this section, or who knowingly advertises the availability of such communications.

(2) The defenses provided in paragraph (1) of this subsection shall not be applicable to a person who provides access or connection to a facility, system, or network engaged in the violation of this section that is owned or controlled by such person.

(3) No employer shall be held liable under this section for the actions of an employee or agent unless the employee's or agent's conduct is within the scope of his or her employment or agency and the employer (A) having knowledge of such conduct, authorizes or ratifies such conduct, or (B) recklessly disregards such conduct.

(4) It is a defense to a prosecution under subsection (a)(1)(B) or (d), or under subsection (a)(2) with respect to the use of a facility for an activity under subsection (a)(1)(B) that a person—

(A) has taken, in good faith, reasonable, effective, and appropriate actions under the circumstances to restrict or prevent access by minors to a communication specified in such subsections, which may involve any appropriate measures to restrict minors from such communications, including any method which is feasible under available technology; or

(B) has restricted access to such communication by requiring use of a verified credit card, debit account, adult access code, or adult personal identification number.

(5) The Commission may describe measures which are reasonable, effective, and appropriate to restrict access to prohibited communications under subsection (d). Nothing in this section authorizes the Commission to enforce, or is intended to provide the Commission with the authority to approve, sanction, or permit, the use of such measures. The Commission shall have no enforcement authority over the failure to utilize such measures. The Commission shall not endorse specific products relating to such measures. The use of such measures shall be admitted as evidence of good faith efforts for purposes of paragraph (5) in any action arising under subsection (d). Nothing in this section shall be construed to treat interactive computer services as common carriers or telecommunications carriers.

(f)(1) No cause of action may be brought in any court or administrative agency against any person on account of any activity that is not in violation of any law punishable by criminal or civil penalty, and that the person has taken in good faith to implement a defense authorized under this section or otherwise to restrict or prevent the transmission of, or access to, a communication specified in this section.

(2) No State or local government may impose any liability for commercial activities or actions by commercial entities, nonprofit libraries, or institutions of higher education in connection with an activity or action described in subsection (a)(2) or (d) that is inconsistent with the treatment of those activities or actions under this section: *Provided, however*, That nothing herein shall preclude any State or local government from enacting and enforcing complementary oversight, liability, and regulatory systems, procedures, and requirements, so long as such systems, procedures, and requirements govern only intrastate services and do not result in the imposition of inconsistent rights, duties or obligations on the provision of interstate services. Nothing in this subsection shall preclude any State or local government from governing conduct not covered by this section.

(g) Nothing in subsection (a), (d), (e), or (f) or in the defenses to prosecution under subsection (a) or (d) shall be construed to affect or limit the application or enforcement of any other Federal law.

(h) INTENTIONAL DISCLOSURE OF NONCONSENSUAL INTIMATE VISUAL DEPICTIONS.—

(1) DEFINITIONS.—In this subsection:

(A) CONSENT.—The term "consent" means an affirmative, conscious, and voluntary authorization made by an individual free from force, fraud, duress, misrepresentation, or coercion.

(B) DIGITAL FORGERY.—The term "digital forgery" means any intimate visual depiction of an identifiable individual created through the use of software, machine learning, artificial intelligence, or any other computer-generated or technological means, including by adapting, modifying, manipulating, or altering an authentic visual depiction, that, when viewed as a whole by a reasonable person, is indistinguishable from an authentic visual depiction of the individual.

(C) IDENTIFIABLE INDIVIDUAL.—The term "identifiable individual" means an individual—

(i) who appears in whole or in part in an intimate visual depiction; and

(ii) whose face, likeness, or other distinguishing characteristic (including a unique birthmark or other recognizable feature) is displayed in connection with such intimate visual depiction.

(D) INTERACTIVE COMPUTER SERVICE.—The term "interactive computer service" has the meaning given the term in section 230.

(E) INTIMATE VISUAL DEPICTION.—The term "intimate visual depiction" has the meaning given such term in section 1309 of the Consolidated Appropriations Act, 2022 (15 U.S.C. 6851).

(F) MINOR.—The term "minor" means any individual under the age of 18 years.

(2) OFFENSE INVOLVING AUTHENTIC INTIMATE VISUAL DEPICTIONS.—

INVOLVING ADULTS.—Except as provided in subparagraph (C), it shall be unlawful for any person, in interstate or foreign commerce, to use an interactive computer serviceto knowingly publish an intimate visual depiction of an identifiable individual who is not a minor if—

(i) the intimate visual depiction was obtained or created under circumstances in which the person knew or reasonably should have known the identifiable individual had a reasonable expectation of privacy;

(ii) what is depicted was not voluntarily exposed by the identifiable individual in a public or commercial setting;

(iii) what is depicted is not a matter of public concern; and

(iv) publication of the intimate visual depiction—

(I) is intended to cause harm; or

(II) causes harm, including psychological, financial, or reputational harm, to the identifiable individual.

(B) INVOLVING MINORS.—Except as provided in subparagraph (C), it shall be unlawful for any person, in interstate or foreign commerce, to use an interactive computer service to knowingly publish an intimate visual depiction of an identifiable individual who is a minor with intent to—

(i) abuse, humiliate, harass, or degrade the minor; or

(ii) arouse or gratify the sexual desire of any person.

(C) EXCEPTIONS.—Subparagraphs (A) and (B) shall not apply to—

(i) a lawfully authorized investigative, protective, or intelligence activity of—

(I) a law enforcement agency of the United States, a State, or a political subdivision of a State; or

(II) an intelligence agency of the United States;

(ii) a disclosure made reasonably and in good faith—

(I) to a law enforcement officer or agency;

(II) as part of a document production or filing associated with a legal proceeding;

(III) as part of medical education, diagnosis, or treatment or for a legitimate medical, scientific, or education purpose;

(IV) in the reporting of unlawful content or unsolicited or unwelcome conduct or in pursuance of a legal, professional, or other lawful obligation; or

(V) to seek support or help with respect to the receipt of an unsolicited intimate visual depiction;

(iii) a disclosure reasonably intended to assist the identifiable individual;

(iv) a person who possesses or publishes an intimate visual depiction of himself or herself engaged in nudity or sexually explicit conduct (as that term is defined in section 2256(2)(A) of title 18, United States Code); or

(v) the publication of an intimate visual depiction that constitutes—

(I) child pornography (as that term is defined in section 2256 of title 18, United States Code); or a visual depiction described in subsection (a) or (b) of section 1466A of title 18, United States Code (relating to obscene visual representations of the sexual abuse of children).

(3)OFFENSE INVOLVING DIGITAL FORGERIES.—

(A) INVOLVING ADULTS.—Except as provided in subparagraph (C), it shall be unlawful for any person, in interstate or foreign commerce, to use an interactive computer service to knowingly publish a digital forgery of an identifiable individual who is not a minor if—

(i) the digital forgery was published without the consent of the identifiable individual;

(ii) what is depicted was not voluntarily exposed by the identifiable individual in a public or commercial setting;

(iii) what is depicted is not a matter of public concern; and

(iv) publication of the digital forgery—

(I) is intended to cause harm; or

(II) causes harm, including psychological, financial, or reputational harm, to the identifiable individual.

(B) INVOLVING MINORS.—Except as provided in subparagraph (C), it shall be unlawful for any person, in interstate or foreign commerce, to use an interactive computer service to knowingly publish a digital forgery of an identifiable individual who is a minor with intent to—

(i) abuse, humiliate, harass, or degrade the minor; or

(ii) arouse or gratify the sexual desire of any person.

(C) EXCEPTIONS.—Subparagraphs (A) and (B) shall not apply to—

(i) a lawfully authorized investigative, protective, or intelligence activity of—

(I) a law enforcement agency of the United States, a State, or a political subdivision of a State; or

(II) an intelligence agency of the United States;

a disclosure made reasonably and in good faith—

(I) to a law enforcement officer or agency;

(II) as part of a document production or filing associated with a legal proceeding;

(III) as part of medical education, diagnosis, or treatment or for a legitimate medical, scientific, or education purpose;

(IV) in the reporting of unlawful content or unsolicited or unwelcome conduct or in pursuance of a legal, professional, or other lawful obligation; or

(V) to seek support or help with respect to the receipt of an unsolicited intimate visual depiction;

(iii) a disclosure reasonably intended to assist the identifiable individual;

(iv) a person who possesses or publishes a digital forgery of himself or herself engaged in nudity or sexually explicit conduct (as that term is defined in section 2256(2)(A) of title 18, United States Code); or the publication of an intimate visual depiction that constitutes—

(I) child pornography (as that term is defined in section 2256 of title 18, United States Code); or

(II) a visual depiction described in subsection (a) or (b) of section 1466A of title 18, United States Code (relating to obscene visual representations of the sexual abuse of children).

(4) PENALTIES.—

(A) OFFENSES INVOLVING ADULTS.—Any person who violates paragraph (2)(A) or (3)(A) shall be fined under title 18, United States Code, imprisoned not more than 2 years, or both.

(B) OFFENSES INVOLVING MINORS.—Any person who violates paragraph (2)(B) or (3)(B) shall be fined under title 18, United States Code, imprisoned not more than 3 years, or both.

(5) RULES OF CONSTRUCTION.—For purposes of paragraphs

(2) and (3)—

(A) the fact that the identifiable individual provided consent for the creation of the intimate visual depiction shall not establish that the individual provided consent for the publication of the intimate visual depiction; and

(B) the fact that the identifiable individual disclosed the intimate visual depiction to another individual shall not establish that the identifiable individual provided consent for the publication of the intimate visual depiction by the person alleged to have violated paragraph (2) or (3), respectively.

(6)THREATS.—

(A) THREATS INVOLVING AUTHENTIC INTIMATE VISUAL DEPICTIONS.—Any person who intentionally threatens to commit an offense under paragraph (2) for the purpose of intimidation, coercion, extortion, or to create mental distress shall be punished as provided in paragraph (4).

(B) THREATS INVOLVING DIGITAL FORGERIES.—

(i) THREATS INVOLVING ADULTS.—Any person who intentionally threatens to commit an offense under paragraph (3)(A) for the purpose of intimidation, coercion, extortion, or to create mental distress shall be fined under title 18, United States Code, imprisoned not more than 18 months, or both.

(ii) THREATS INVOLVING MINORS.—Any person who intentionally threatens to commit an offense under paragraph (3)(B) for the purpose of intimidation, coercion, extortion, or to create mental distress shall be fined under title 18, United States Code, imprisoned not more than 30 months, or both.

(7) FORFEITURE.—

(A) IN GENERAL.—The court, in imposing a sentence on any person convicted of a violation of paragraph (2) or (3), shall order, in addition to any other sentence imposed and irrespective of any provision of State law, that the person forfeit to the United States—any material distributed in violation of that paragraph;

(i) the person's interest in property, real or personal, constituting or derived from any gross proceeds of the violation, or any property traceable to such property, obtained or retained directly or indirectly as a result of the violation; and

(ii) any personal property of the person used, or intended to be used, in any manner or part, to commit or to facilitate the commission of the violation.

(B) PROCEDURES.—Section 413 of the Controlled Substances Act (21 U.S.C. 853), with the exception of subsections (a) and (d), shall apply to the criminal forfeiture of property under subparagraph (A).

(8) RESTITUTION.—The court shall order restitution for an offense under paragraph (2) or (3) in the same manner as under section 2264 of title 18, United States Code.

(9) RULE OF CONSTRUCTION.—Nothing in this subsection shall be construed to limit the application of any other relevant law, including section 2252 of title 18, United States Code.

ø(h)¿ (i) DEFINITIONS.—For purposes of this section—

(1) The use of the term "telecommunications device" in this section—

(A) shall not impose new obligations on broadcasting station licensees and cable operators covered by obscenity and indecency provisions elsewhere in this Act;

(B) does not include an interactive computer service; and

(C) in the case of subparagraph (C) of subsection (a)(1), includes any device or software that can be used to originate telecommunications or other types of communications that are transmitted, in whole or in part, by the Internet (as such term is defined in section 1104 of the Internet Tax Freedom Act (47 U.S.C. 151 note)).

(2) The term "interactive computer service" has the meaning provided in section 230(f)(2).

(3) The term "access software" means software (including client or server software) or enabling tools that do not create or provide the content of the communication but that allow a user to do any one or more of the following:

(A) filter, screen, allow, or disallow content;

(B) pick, choose, analyze, or digest content; or

(C) transmit, receive, display, forward, cache, search, subset, organize, reorganize, or translate content.

(4) The term "institution of higher education" has the meaning provided in section 101 of the Higher Education Act of 1965.

(5) The term "library" means a library eligible for participation in State-based plans for funds under title III of the Library Services and Construction Act (20 U.S.C. 355e et seq.).

* * * * * *

Minority Views

In H.R. 633, the TAKE IT DOWN Act, Congress entrusts the Federal Trade Commission (FTC) with delivering on a promise to provide recourse to those victimized by bad actors who have exploited advancing technology including generative AI that can depict vulnerable individuals in sexually explicit situations that never occurred, and ubiquitous online social media that allows images to be distributed to an entire contact list at the push of a button, destroying reputations and lives in the process.

When Congress created the FTC, it recognized the need for a government entity that could protect Americans faced with enormous and powerful corporations focused solely on pursuit of profit. Congress recognized that a dynamic marketplace with constant advances in business practices and technology required the development of specialized expertise, and that to have trust and legitimacy in the eyes of consumers, markets, and the courts, such an agency would require independence and ideological balance, ensuring a fair hearing, transparency, and accountability.

This is why Congress specifically constructed the FTC as a multimember Commission led by Commissioners representing more than one political party, with terms that extended longer than those of Representatives, Senators, or Presidents. To avoid political pressure from a presidential administration, the FTC Act is clear that once appointed by the President and confirmed by the Senate, no Commissioner can be dismissed without due cause, explicitly specified as "inefficiency, neglect of duty, or malfeasance in office."

For more than a century, the FTC has lived up to its statutory obligation as an independent agency protecting competition and consumers. Recognizing the FTC's good work, Congress has given it additional statutory authority over a wide range of consumer protection areas.

It is, therefore, unconscionable that in hearings and markup regarding H.R. 633 and the online dangers allowed to proliferate by Big Tech, where the role for the FTC to responsibly monitor and bring accountability to rogue corporations could not be more apparent or urgent, the majority abandoned its duty to defend the Commission and its leaders against clear ideological animus.

Commissioner Rebecca Kelly Slaughter, who President Trump has illegally attempted to fire without cause, was called as a witness in the March 26, 2025, hearing entitled "The World Wild Web: Examining Harms Online," where she forcefully argued for the FTC's important duty to act on the very harms under discussion in an independent and transparent manner. Commissioner Slaughter recounted how in her long service to the Commission, the agency had vigorously pursued this mission across Presidential administrations with all the authorities granted by Congress. Commissioner Slaughter's testimony strongly made the case that Congress would be right to entrust an independent FTC, and its Commissioners, with once again protecting vulnerable Americans and that they would continue to do so through their full statutory terms regardless of what political party might be in power at the time.

Despite this, the majority insisted in its hearing announcements and at the hearing itself on referring to Ms. Slaughter as a "former" Commissioner, inexplicably attempting to legitimize the unlawful actions of a President pursuing a nakedly political agenda by claiming the ability to fire independent FTC commissioners at a whim, directly contravening established law and precedent.

At the April 8, 2025 Committee markup of H.R. 633, Representative Soto introduced an amendment to allow the Committee members to vote to address this clear law violation and reaffirm their Constitutional role as a co-equal branch of government by conditioning the effective date of H.R. 633 on the recognition that the President's unlawful attempt to fire Commissioner Slaughter and her Colleague Commissioner Alvaro Bedoya without cause was contrary to law and that these Commissioners were entitled to continue to serve out their terms, ensuring transparency and legitimacy for the agency tasked with enforcing the critical notice and takedown provisions of the bill.

The minority also introduced several amendments to make H.R. 633 stronger, clearer, and to address areas of the bill where insufficient consideration was given to the possibility of loopholes and unintended consequences that might threaten the good the bill aims to do for victims. The majority made clear, however, that it was unwilling to consider amendments to H.R. 633 because it intended to adopt the exact same version of the Take it Down Act that has already moved through the Senate.

The goals of H.R. 633 are laudable, but rather than rushing this bill through the Committee the majority should have taken more care to clarify and strengthen the bill and to defend the statutory independence of the agency that it intends to enforce the notice and takedown provisions of this Act, to ensure that the FTC can do its work without fear or favor.

FRANK PALLONE, Jr.,
Ranking Member.

Chapter 7

Deepfake Task Force Act*

Committee on Homeland Security and Governmental Affairs

I. Purpose and Summary

S. 2559, the Deepfake Task Force Act, requires the Secretary of Homeland Security to convene a task force to examine how to reduce the proliferation of deepfakes and differentiate these digital forgeries from authentic images, video, text, or audio. Task Force members will be experts in artificial intelligence, media manipulation, digital forensics, and other related subjects and come from the federal government, higher education, and private or nonprofit organizations. The task force will develop a coordinated plan to reduce the proliferation and impact of deepfakes, including through new digital content provenance standards and technologies. The findings and recommendations of the task force will be submitted to the President and Congress through an interim report and a final report.

II. Background and the Need for Legislation

Deepfakes are highly realistic images and sounds that are created through artificial intelligence (AI) and machine learning (ML). Deepfake creators can use deepfake technology to manipulate media and replace an actual person's

* This is an edited, reformatted and augmented version of Senate Report 117–114, Calendar No. 382, dated May 24, 2022.

In: The Deepfake Dilemma
Editor: Ruben Faulkner
ISBN: 979-8-90134-122-3

image or voice with artificial likenesses or voices. As the software underpinning these technologies becomes easier to acquire and use, the dissemination of deepfake content across trusted media platforms has the potential to undermine national security and erode public trust in our democracy, among other nefarious impacts.

The threat that deepfakes could pose if used in misinformation campaigns is well known and well-documented. The Congressional Research Service (CRS) has noted that "[s]tate adversaries or politically motivated individuals could release falsified videos of elected officials or other public figures making incendiary comments or behaving inappropriately. Doing so could, in turn, erode public trust, negatively affect public discourse, or even sway an election."[1] Instances of such sophisticated misinformation have already been reported: fictitious journalists with invented backgrounds and AI-generated avatars have proliferated opinion pieces on various issues related to the Middle East,[2] and Taiwanese authorities have identified signs that China used AI-powered misinformation to interfere with Taiwan's 2020 elections.[3] Testimony before Congress has further highlighted the national security challenges of deepfakes and artificial intelligence.[4]

The 116th Congress responded to the threat of deepfakes with a variety of legislation, including Section 589F of the FY 2021 National Defense Authorization Act (P.L. 116–293), which requires the Department of Defense to complete an "intelligence assessment of the threat posed by foreign government and non-state actors creating or using machine-manipulated media (commonly referred to as 'deep fakes')."[5] The Identifying Outputs of Generative Adversarial Networks Act (P.L. 116–258) directed the National Science Foundation (NSF) and the National Institute of Standards and Technology (NIST) to support research on generative adversarial networks, which are the systems that produce deepfakes. The Deepfake Report Act (P.L. 116–283) requires the Science and Technology Directorate in the Department of Homeland Security to report at specific intervals on the state of digital

---

[1] Congressional Research Service, *Deep Fakes and National Security* (IF11333) (Jun. 8, 2021).

[2] *An Online Propaganda Campaign Used AI-generated Headshots to Create Fake Journalists,* The Verge (Jul. 7, 2020) (https://www.theverge.com/2020/7/7/21315861/ai-generated-headshots-profile-pictures-fake-journalists-daily-beast-investigation).

[3] *China Uses Taiwan for AI Target Practice to Influence Elections,* The Australian (Jan. 5, 2020) (https://www.theaustralian.com.au/world/the-times/china-uses-taiwan-for-ai-target-practice-to-influence-elections/news-story/57499d2650d4d359a3857688d416d1e5).

[4] Permanent Select Committee on Intelligence, *National Security Challenges of Artificial Intelligence, Manipulated Media, and Deepfakes*, 116th Cong. (Jun. 13, 2019).

[5] National Defense Authorization Act of 2021, Pub. L. 116–283, Sec. 589F(b)(8) (2021).

content forgery technology.[6] While these laws provide important first steps in understanding deepfakes and their uses, they do not address the need for coordinated strategies to stem the proliferation of misinformation powered by deepfakes, including through digital content prove nance technologies that could help distinguish authentic media from deepfakes.[7]

In response to the challenges of misinformation, private sector efforts are underway to develop standards to certify the authenticity and provenance of audiovisual content.[8] Further, the National Security Commission on Artificial Intelligence has stated that this technology area is ripe for public-private partnership.[9] The task force created by S. 2559 will include experts from the government, private sector, and higher education who will work together to produce a coordinated plan to reduce the proliferation and impact of digital misinformation through deepfakes.

III. Legislative History

Senator Rob Portman (R–OH) introduced S. 2559, the Deepfake Task Force Act, on July 29, 2021, with Chairman Gary Peters (D– MI) as cosponsor. The bill was referred to the Committee on Homeland Security and Governmental Affairs.

The Committee considered S. 2559 at a business meeting on August 4, 2021. The bill was ordered reported favorably en bloc by voice vote with Senators Peters, Carper, Hassan, Sinema, Rosen, Padilla, Ossoff, Portman, Johnson, Lankford, Romney, Scott, and Hawley present.

---

[6] S. 2065, 116th Cong. (2019).

[7] For example, the National Security Commission on Artificial Intelligence (NSCAI) recommended the creation of a task force, such as the one created by S. 2559, to study digital content authenticity and provenance. National Security Commission on Artificial Intelligence, *Final Report* (March 1, 2021), at 49.

[8] *Id.; see also* Coalition for Content Provenance and Authenticity, Home Page (https://c2pa.org) (accessed Oct. 21, 2021).

[9] National Security Commission on Artificial Intelligence, *Final Report* (March 1, 2021), at 49.

IV. Section-by-Section Analysis of The Bill, as Reported

Section 1. Short Title

The short title of the bill is the Deepfake Task Force Act.

Section 2. National Deepfake and Digital Provenance Task Force

This section establishes a task force on deepfakes and digital provenance. The task force has 12 members (four members each from government, academia, and the private sector), and is chaired by the Department of Homeland Security (DHS) and the Office of Science and Technology Policy (OSTP).

The purpose of the task force is to reduce the proliferation and impact of deepfakes, with a specific focus on the development of standards for digital provenance. The task force will assemble experts to help develop necessary provenance standards to ensure digital provenance technology is accessible, interoperable with different cameras and internet platforms, and privacy-focused.

The task force will also propose research projects to improve the detection of deepfakes, policy changes to reduce the proliferation of deepfakes online, models for public-private partnerships to fight disinformation, and metrics to determine the success of technologies at reducing the proliferation of deepfakes.

The task force will generally be staffed by detailees from other agencies. Where the task force seeks to hire an individual outside of government, that individual would be paid by their parent organization.

Finally, the task force will produce an interim report within one year after establishment, and a final report within 180 days after the interim report. The task force shall terminate 90 days after the final report.

V. Evaluation of Regulatory Impact

Pursuant to the requirements of paragraph 11(b) of rule XXVI of the Standing Rules of the Senate, the Committee has considered the regulatory impact of this bill and determined that the bill will have no regulatory impact within the meaning of the rules. The Committee agrees with the Congressional Budget

Office's statement that the bill contains no intergovernmental or private-sector mandates as defined in the Unfunded Mandates Reform Act (UMRA) and would impose no costs on state, local, or tribal governments.

VI. Congressional Budget Office Cost Estimate

U.S. Congress, Congressional Budget Office,
Washington, DC, January 11, 2022.

Hon. GARY C. PETERS,
Chairman,
Committee on Homeland Security and Governmental Affairs,
U.S. Senate,
Washington, DC.

DEAR MR. CHAIRMAN: The Congressional Budget Office has prepared the enclosed cost estimate for S. 2559, the Deepfake Task Force Act.

If you wish further details on this estimate, we will be pleased to provide them. The CBO staff contact is Lindsay Wylie.

Sincerely,
Phillip L. Swagel,
Director.

Enclosure.

S. 2559, Deepfake Task Force Act
As ordered reported by the Senate Committee on Homeland Security and Governmental Affairs on August 4, 2021

By Fiscal Year, Millions of Dollars	2022	2022-2026	2022-2031
Direct Spending (Outlays)	0	0	0
Revenues	0	0	0
Increase or Decrease (-) in the Deficit	0	0	0
Spending Subject to Appropriation (Outlays)	1	3	not estimated

Statutory pay-as-you-go procedures apply?	No	Mandate Effects	
Increases on-budget deficits in any of the four consecutive 10-year periods beginning in 2032?	No	Contains intergovernmental mandate?	No
		Contains private-sector mandate?	No

S. 2559 would require the Department of Homeland Security (DHS) to establish a task force to address digital content forgeries, also known as "deepfakes." These forgeries manipulate digital content, such as videos, with the intent to mislead the viewer. The task force would investigate the feasibility of deploying standards and technologies for verifying the origin and history of digital content. The bill also would require DHS to develop a national strategy to address threats posed by digital content forgeries in consultation with federal agencies and private and non-profit organizations. The task force would submit an initial report to the Congress on its findings and recommendations after one year, transmit a final report six months later, and terminate three months after the final report is submitted.

The task force would consist of 12 members, including two chair-persons from relevant federal agencies. The other 10 members would include two additional federal employees and eight representatives from non-profit or private organizations or institutions of higher education. The bill would allow members to be reimbursed for travel expenses. Using information about the cost of similar entities, CBO estimates DHS would need $3 million over the 2022–2026 period for staff, travel, and other administrative expenses to operate the task force. Such spending would be subject to the availability of appropriated funds.

The CBO staff contact for this estimate is Lindsay Wylie. The estimate was reviewed by Leo Lex, Deputy Director of Budget Analysis.

VII. Changes in Existing Law Made by the Bill, as Reported

Because S. 2559 would not repeal or amend any provision of current law, it would make no changes in existing law within the meaning of clauses (a) and (b) of paragraph 12 of rule XXVI of the Standing Rules of the Senate.

Index

A

activism, 13
artificial intelligence, 1, 5, 30, 31, 36, 39, 57, 62, 63, 77, 84, 104, 113, 114

B

broadband, 98
bullying, 34

C

Catalog of Federal Domestic Assistance, 95
censorship, 32
child pornography, 18, 30, 50, 99, 102, 105, 106
childhood sexual abuse, 48
China, 50, 53, 68, 73, 114
civil action, 15, 64, 70, 71, 101
civil law, 36, 37, 46, 65
cloning, 9, 11
Code of Federal Regulations, 98
coercion, 104, 107
communication, 34, 99, 100, 101, 102, 103, 108
Communications Act, 96, 98, 99
Communications Act of 1934, 96, 98, 99
constituents, 8, 28
constitution, 44, 67
constitutional challenges, 38
constitutional issues, 38
consumer protection, 109
Controlled Substances Act, 108
counterfeiting, 41
criminal behavior, 29, 79
critical thinking, 10
cultural heritage, 8
culture, 15
cyberbullying, 9
cybersecurity, 3, 10

D

database, 85
defamation, 41, 44, 47
detection system, 14
discrimination, 11
distress, 40, 107
distribution, 30, 31, 33, 41, 57, 65, 67, 69, 70, 90, 102

E

education, 10, 12, 14, 34, 37, 42, 57, 103, 105, 106, 109, 113, 115, 118
educational institutions, 34
educational system, 49
election, 12, 14, 32, 53, 63, 64, 67, 68, 74, 78, 114
encryption, 3
exploitation, 35, 36, 40, 50, 54

F

facial expression, 85
First Amendment, 16, 20, 38, 40, 41, 45, 51, 67, 86
foreign intelligence, 78
Fourteenth Amendment, 44

H

human right(s), 10, 12

M

machine learning, 77, 84, 104, 113

N

National Center for Missing and Exploited Children, 33, 35, 92, 95
National Defense Authorization Act, 8, 79, 114
neural network(s), 77

P

parents, 15, 34, 42, 53, 56
penalties, 15, 41, 68, 69, 75, 94, 96, 97, 100
performing artists, 66
permit, 65, 74, 103
perpetrators, 31, 37, 46, 58
photographs, 2, 29, 30, 34, 36, 38, 91
platform, 7, 8, 31, 36, 52, 55, 58, 74, 75, 94, 97, 98
pleasure, 13, 17, 57
police, 14, 34, 45
policy, vii, 13, 30, 43, 63, 64, 67, 68, 116
political party, 109, 110
precedent, 41, 110
predators, 91
prevention, 37
private sector, 4, 5, 8, 14, 73, 81, 115, 116
profit, 109, 118
programming, 66
proliferation, 4, 30, 31, 40, 113, 115, 116
protection, 17, 41, 53, 109
psychological distress, 40
public awareness, 10
public concern, 104, 106
public education, 12
public figures, 78, 114
public policy, 13, 63, 64, 67, 68

R

race, 38, 46, 50
radio, 47, 66
rape, 28, 30, 42
reality, 2, 7, 24
recognition, 6, 21, 110
regulations, 65, 69, 75, 86
regulatory systems, 103
relief, 57, 64, 65
researchers, 32, 78
resources, 36, 41, 46, 48, 53
response, 3, 24, 25, 34, 60, 115
restitution, 108
restrictions, 20, 81
retribution, 20
rights, vii, 10, 12, 13, 51, 53, 103
risk(s), 3, 7, 8, 11, 39, 40, 48, 49, 64
rules, 19, 20, 37, 67, 116
Russia, 3, 53, 78

S

safety, 18, 35, 37, 55, 66, 82, 91
school, 2, 4, 9, 10, 13, 32, 33, 34, 35, 37, 40, 42, 43, 45, 48, 49, 50, 52, 53
security(ies), vii, 2, 9, 53, 61, 63, 64, 66, 73, 77, 81, 82, 83, 86, 114
security threats, 2
servers, 55
sex, 13, 21, 22, 36, 45, 54
sexual abuse, 2, 11, 31, 36, 38, 39, 45, 48, 50, 54, 55, 56, 105, 107
shame, 13, 42, 49
social network, 73, 75
social upheaval, 14
society, 9, 86, 90
software, 9, 12, 52, 78, 102, 104, 108, 114
solution, 15, 24, 31, 57
standing rules, 116, 118
state laws, 15
statutory authority, 109
suicide, 29, 40, 48, 91
surveillance, 12, 24

T

target, 39, 51, 114
tariff, 96
technological advancement, 31
technological advances, 11
technology(ies), vii, 2, 3, 4, 5, 6, 7, 8, 9, 10, 11, 12, 13, 14, 15, 16, 19, 21, 22, 23, 28, 29, 30, 32, 36, 37, 39, 40, 42, 43, 44, 46, 49, 50, 51, 58, 61, 62, 63, 68, 73, 77, 78, 79, 80, 81, 83, 84, 85, 86, 87, 90, 103, 109, 113, 114, 115, 116, 118
telecommunications, 99, 100, 102, 103, 108
territorial, 63, 64, 65, 72
theft, 2, 63, 64
threats, vii, 2, 32, 61, 97, 118
trafficking, 45
training, 32, 37, 56, 57, 85, 86
transactions, 59
transmission, 99, 102, 103
transparency, 4, 6, 7, 8, 12, 109, 110
trauma, 43, 48, 49, 50
treatment, 89, 103, 105, 106

U

Ukraine, 2, 3, 8, 18
United States, 35, 44, 51, 53, 55, 61, 66, 67, 68, 69, 70, 71, 72, 73, 74, 75, 83, 88, 91, 92, 100, 101, 102, 105, 106, 107, 108

V

variations, 11
victimization, 35
victims, 17, 28, 29, 30, 31, 33, 34, 40, 42, 44, 49, 51, 55, 57, 58, 59, 60, 61, 91, 110
videos, 2, 4, 7, 9, 13, 14, 15, 20, 23, 29, 30, 40, 43, 46, 47, 48, 52, 54, 59, 75, 78, 79, 84, 89, 90, 98, 114, 118
violence, 7, 13, 44, 48, 63, 64, 68, 79

W

war, 3, 56, 78
war crimes, 78
wire fraud, 63, 64
work environment, 90

Y

yield, 3, 5, 6, 16, 20, 30, 32, 34, 43, 44, 45, 48, 52, 56, 58
young people, 4, 54
young women, 4